Stanbrook Abbey

Stanbrook Abbey

Pamela Hurle

Stanbrook Abbey
Pamela Hurle

Published by Aspect Design

Designed, printed and bound by Aspect Design
89 Newtown Road, Malvern, Worcs. WR14 1PD
United Kingdom
Tel: 01684 561567
E-mail: allan@aspect-design.net
Website: www.aspect-design.net

A copy of this book has been deposited
with the British Library Board

Cover photograph courtesy of Andrew Grant and Neil Styles.

Stanbrook Abbey title text based on the font Cancelleresca Bastarda
by the typographer Jan van Krimpen which was used by the nuns
during Stanbrook Abbey Press's hayday.

ISBN 978-1-908832-82-5

CONTENTS

List of Illustrations 7

Preface 9

Acknowledgements 11

1. The Early History of Stanbrook Abbey 13
   - Benedictines in Flanders at Douai and Cambrai 14
   - The More Family 15
   - Early Problems in Cambrai 16
   - Dame Catherine Gascoigne 18
   - A New House in Paris 22

2. Paradise Achieved—and Lost—in Cambrai 25
   - Building Paradise 25
   - The French Revolution 28
   - Safety in England 33

3. At Home in Stanbrook 37
   - Stanbrook Hall 37
   - Could the Abbey Survive? 41
   - Changing Attitudes in England 46

4. Change, Expansion and Growing Confidence 48
   - Impact of the Oxford Movement in the Church of England 48
   - Edward Welby Pugin 50
   - Consolidation and Success 56

5. Enclosed Nuns with Unenclosed Minds 59

Dame Laurentia McLachlan 1866–1953 59

Dame Felicitas Corrigan 1908–2003 61

Other Friendships Through the Monastic Grille 63

The Stanbrook Press 64

6. Changes in the Roman Catholic Church and to Stanbrook 67

A Window Opened by Pope John XXIII 67

Practical and Financial Considerations at Stanbrook 68

Removal to Yorkshire 70

Survival 75

Appendix One. The Origins of Christian Monasticism 76

St Benedict of Nursia c.480–c.543 76

The Rule Devised by St Benedict for Monastic Life 78

Personal Demands and Widespread Effects of the Rule of St Benedict 81

Appendix Two. Medieval Religious Supremacy and the Rise of National Feeling 84

The Power of the Medieval Church in Western Europe 84

Spiritual and Material Power of the Church 85

Challenges to the Church's Authority 86

Why Were Roman Catholics in England Viewed with Suspicion for Centuries? 87

Refusal to Accept a Roman Catholic Monarch 87

The Jacobites 88

Glossary 91

Bibliography 95

Literary Works Associated with the Life and Work of the Stanbrook Community 98

LIST OF ILLUSTRATIONS

Dame Gertrude More (Helen More) 15
Two views of the original foundation at Cambrai 16
Dame Catherine Gascoigne 18
Reliquary and relics of the Carmelite martyrs of Compiègne 31
Salford Hall 35
Part of an 1822 map showing the position of Stanbrook 38
Stanbrook Hall in 1835 39
Stanbrook Abbey in 1838 39
Inside Charles Day's chapel in 1900 40
Nuns with children at Stanbrook, 1868 42
Visitors to Stanbrook, 1868 43
Nuns' burial ground in 1868 44
Stanbrook Abbey school advertisement c.1840 45
Late nineteenth-century nuns in Stanbrook garden 47
Stanbrook's church exterior in 1871 51
The tower at Stanbrook Abbey in sunlight 51
Interior view of Stanbrook's church, 1871 52
Stanbrook's church interior in the twenty-first century 53
Father Laurence Shepherd 54
Dame Gertrude d'Aurillac Dubois 54
Dame Cecilia Heywood 55
Margaret McLachlan in her youth 60
The mature Dame Laurentia . . . . .

The monastic grille at Stanbrook Abbey which emphasised enclosure 60
Clothing ceremony of a nun at Stanbrook Abbey 66
Aerial view of cloister garth with the shadow
of the tower at Stanbrook Abbey 69
Inside Stanbrook's church, view to the northwest 69
The refectory at Stanbrook Abbey 70
A corridor in Stanbrook Abbey 71
Via crucis cloister at Stanbrook Abbey 71
The summer house in the grounds of Stanbrook Abbey, 1874 72
Stanbrook Abbey's summer house in the early twenty-first century 72
The retreat house at Stanbrook Abbey 73
Stanbrook Abbey at Wass 73

PREFACE

This book tells a remarkable story of English Roman Catholic nuns. Established in Flanders nearly four hundred years ago and hounded during the French Revolution, the community sought a home in England, eventually settling for 170 years at Stanbrook in the small Worcestershire hamlet of Callow End in Powick, near Malvern, until its recent removal to Yorkshire.

Its history is, I believe, best seen as part of our national—indeed international—religious heritage, just as I am sure that local history cannot be fully understood without being set in a national context. The aims, perils and excitements of the nuns' story become more remarkable when set in context so there are two appendices to provide some background material. The first of these outlines the development of monasticism in Western Europe and the second offers some thoughts on the conflict between the all-embracing power of the pre-reformation church and the ambitions of an emergent national government seeking political control. There is also a glossary of relevant terms.

The history of monasticism first appealed to me as a sixth-former sixty years ago. It has long lain at the back of my mind as a subject to explore again when, as I naively assumed, retirement would yield the necessary time. Recently the removal of the Benedictine Stanbrook community from Callow End led to the development of a greater sense of urgency about the project.

A feature which emerged as the story of the nuns unfolded was the skill with which change has, over centuries, been embraced without loss of respect for, and pursuit of, ancient traditions of worship and service. Closely regulated and requiring submission of one's own wishes to the perceived needs of the community and, indeed, of the world, monastic life is not a retreat from problems and hardship.

ACKNOWLEDGEMENTS

A short history of Stanbrook, written in 1925 by Dame Laurentia MacLachlan, was made available to me by local historian Christine Bannister. This book inspired me to do more research and ultimately led to *Stanbrook Abbey* becoming my latest publication on the local history of the Malvern area. A project full of interest for me, it could not have appeared in its present form without a good deal of help from others.

Although the Stanbrook nuns are now based in Yorkshire their archivist, Sister Scholastica, has been most encouraging in her correspondence and, having read my manuscript, pointed me in the right direction when I erred in my interpretation. On top of her many other duties in the Abbey she has the responsibility of sorting all its records, until this year held in storage after the move from Worcestershire, and has given up precious time to enable the reproduction of images of material in the Abbey archive, for which I thank her and the community. Illustrations are vital to bring this subject alive and I have been fortunate indeed to be permitted to use some excellent pictures. From the start I owed a debt of thanks to Michael Hill, who allowed me to use not only some of his images of the community's archives but also photographs from the Conservation Plan which he produced when the decision was made to put the Stanbrook estate on the market. Andrew

Grant, the estate agent who negotiated the sale of Stanbrook, produced an illustrated brochure with photographs by Neil Styles, and I thank both of them, too, for allowing me to use these lovely images.

Peter Smith, founder and artistic director of the Autumn in Malvern Festival, has encouraged me in this project, offered sound advice whenever I met a problem and invited me to speak and to launch this book during the 2015 Festival, for all of which I thank him. Aspect Design's professionalism, always combined with a friendly, helpful manner, makes it a pleasure to work with them and I thank them for their never-failing good humour.

Finally, but not least, I thank my husband who has for nearly half a century supported me through many local history projects on which I could never have embarked without his support and encouragement. He has again played the difficult role of critical friend, reading and commenting on my (nearly final) text. This led to some amendments but any remaining errors are my own.

Pamela Hurle
August 2015

CHAPTER ONE
The Early History of Stanbrook Abbey

At the edge of Callow End village in the Worcestershire parish of Powick is Stanbrook Abbey with its impressive neo-Gothic buildings designed by Edward Welby Pugin. For 170 years it was the home of an enclosed order of Benedictine nuns who in 2009 moved to Wass in Yorkshire. Their former home at Callow End is now open to all, as its purchasers, the Clarenco Group, have restored it in a sensitive manner to produce a luxury hotel.

The Benedictine community which went to Stanbrook in 1838 can trace its history back to early seventeenth-century Flanders. This book tells of its struggles and success. Background information on the Benedictine order and on the political climate which caused the Stanbrook nuns to found their abbey in Flanders is contained in two appendices at the back. This enables their story to be told with the immediacy which it deserves, for it is a very sobering history.

In the seventeenth century numerous English Roman Catholic women struggled to found a total of twenty-one religious communities,[1] some Benedictine, but it was unrealistic to expect to set them up in England, in view of the social, political and religious prejudices at that time.

1 David Lunn, *The English Benedictines 1540–1688* (Burns and Oates, 1980) p. 198.

Henry VIII's break from Rome in the 1530s and the ensuing political and religious history of the sixteenth and seventeenth centuries had led to English distrust of anything that smacked of 'popery' and Catholic ritual. So, when new religious houses were founded for English monks and nuns, sites in Flanders and northern France—not too far from home—had particular appeal. Such houses in continental Europe, although largely autonomous, came under the umbrella of the English Benedictine Congregation which had existed in medieval times and was revived in the early seventeenth century. The Congregation's overview of religious houses has helped and guided the individual communities for centuries and continues to do so.

Benedictines in Flanders at Douai and Cambrai

One group of English and Welsh Benedictine monks set up a monastery at Douai in 1606 but had to leave after the French Revolution led to a French dissolution of the monasteries even more brutal than the English dissolution had been. Nearly twenty years after its arrival in England the Douai community settled in Somerset at Downside in 1814, but during its years in Douai it had helped to support several generations of English Catholics who wished to pursue the monastic life but could not do so in their native country. Among those assisted by the Douai monks was the community of nuns who eventually came to Stanbrook. After some weeks in Douai the women went to Cambrai, then, like Douai, in Flanders, which became part of France in the late seventeenth century. This political change in national borders was to prove significant for the nuns: they were in Cambrai for 170 years and left only when the horrors of the French Revolution made escape to England imperative in the 1790s.

The More Family

The story of the Cambrai nuns started in the summer of 1623 when Cresacre More left England with eight young female postulants—people wanting to take up monastic life. Cresacre More was the great-grandson of Thomas More, Henry VIII's Lord Chancellor, and inherited much of his great-grandfather's property. Cresacre More was the father of seventeen-year-old Helen, the leader of the postulants, and he gave financial backing without which the expedition could never have set off. This financial support explains and reinforces the special gratitude that the Stanbrook nuns have always felt towards Thomas More and his descendants. Once highly valued by Henry VIII, Thomas More was executed in 1535 because he opposed the king's religious policy; he was canonised four hundred years later by Pope Pius XI. Such steadfastness to Roman Catholicism was also a hallmark of More's descendant Cresacre More and many of his family. Helen More, a spirited, fun-loving girl born only seventy-one years after Thomas More's execution, did not at first seem a likely candidate for the religious life but felt gratitude and affection for both her father and the Catholic priest Dom Benet Jones: he was her confessor and the man she regarded as her spiritual father, his title of 'Dom' being given to spiritual leaders such as professed monks in certain orders. These debts of gratitude caused young Helen, at an impressionable age, to take on the responsibility of leading the other young women to Douai, on a journey full of uncertainties.

Helen More, leader of the postulants who left England in 1623. Her name in religion was Dame Gertrude More. This portrayal does not reflect her reputation as lively and fun-loving! *Image courtesy of Stanbrook Abbey.*

Monastic site at the rue des Anglaises (*left*), remains of the cloister (*right*). The first permanent home of the community of nuns who eventually came to Stanbrook was an old abbey in Cambrai, renovated for them in the 1620s and richly embellished over the next 170 years. French Revolutionary forces evicted them in 1793. By the early twentieth century, when these pictures were taken, the street was known as the rue des Anglaises—the street of the English women. The buildings were then scarcely recognisable as their home, once referred to as Paradise. *Pictures by J. M. Dailliez, courtesy of Stanbrook Abbey.*

Early Problems in Cambrai

Dom Benet Jones, who became the spiritual leader of this group of young women, took them to Douai where they stayed for several weeks until in September they travelled about fifteen miles to Cambrai. After temporary lodging while an old abbey in an acre of ground at Fémy on the outskirts of Cambrai was made habitable, they entered the still dilapidated building on Christmas Eve 1623, local builders predicting that its four bare walls would not stand for more than thirty years. Three experienced Dames—the title given to professed nuns who had taken their vows—came from an English Benedictine house at Brussels to guide them in their new life in the Cambrai house dedicated to Our Lady of Comfort. The small community was put in the charge of Dame Frances Gawen, who had been a professed nun for twenty-eight years. The other two experienced Dames were Pudentiana Deacons and Viviana Yaxley, who was novice mistress with special responsibility for those new to the religious life. After some initial difficulty in the appointment of a suitable confessor and spiritual guide Dom Augustine Baker, a man known for his learning and asceticism, held this position until 1631. Other chaplains were also appointed, necessarily male since the Roman Catholic Church does not ordain women as priests—and only a priest may hear confessions and celebrate Mass.

Nine postulants, including Catherine Gascoigne, who had joined the original group and was to become an outstanding abbess, took vows a year later on 1 January 1625, each being given her 'name in religion' by which she was subsequently known. The youth of some of them is astonishing to our modern perceptions. Helen More (Dame Gertrude) was now nearly nineteen; Margaret Vavasour (Dame Lucy) was sixteen and her sister Catherine, who came a year later, was also sixteen when she entered the religious life. Gentle and earnest Anne Morgan, (Dame Benet) who entered at twenty, sadly lost her mind and died at the age of thirty-six. Frances Watson (Dame Mary) was only fifteen when she entered: talented and prayerful she lived from 1608 to 1646. Anne More and Grace More (Dame Agnes), like Helen More, were related to Thomas More. There were two lay sisters, who did not take the full vows of professed or choir nuns: Mary Hoskins, able and intelligent, served for over forty years and Martha Millar, whose family was well-to-do, died in 1631 aged forty-three after using money which a former suitor wished to settle on her to found a Catholic education charity rather than spend it on herself by becoming a Dame.

From the first there were problems regarding the religious practices that were to be adopted. Great tact and strength were needed to find a spiritual guide who would help the women to find a suitable form for their contemplative life, and Father Baker was initially hampered by what he called 'the witty tongue and animosity' of the irrepressible Dame Gertrude, whom he eventually won over. He had somewhat controversially revived medieval forms of contemplation, which were different from Jesuit spiritual exercises which had become popular in monastic circles. The conflict which ensued was bitter—as history has shown religious divisions so often are.

Dame Catherine Gascoigne

Dame Catherine Gascoigne, from a staunchly Roman Catholic family, became abbess at Cambrai at the age of twenty-nine. For forty years she provided the strong leadership the new community needed. She died in May 1676. *Image courtesy of Stanbrook Abbey.*

In 1629, five years after the house was started, their first abbess and mentor, Dame Frances, was succeeded as abbess by Dame Catherine Gascoigne, who unusually retained her original baptismal name. The Gascoigne family was to play an important part in the history of the community which she now headed. Although the three experienced nuns, who had come from Brussels to help in the foundation at Cambrai, could have gone back to Brussels they all wanted to stay at Cambrai, where Dame Frances died in 1640 and Dame Pudentiana in 1645, both aged sixty-three.[1] Dame Viviana did go back to Brussels in 1650, when the Cambrai house was in serious financial straits and finding difficulty in supporting all their nuns.

Dame Catherine Gascoigne was six years older and more self-disciplined than Helen More (Dame Gertrude), who had,

1 Catholic Record Society, *Miscellanea*, vol. VIII (1913), pp. 76–78.

of course, been the original leader of the postulants. Dame Gertrude, affectionate, intelligent and sociable, died from smallpox four years later at the age of twenty-seven. Dame Catherine was repeatedly re-elected as abbess for forty years (except for a period of four years when she was sent to reform another religious house of French nuns in Cambrai) from 1629 to 1673. Born in 1600, she had been a great beauty until at the age of nineteen she caught smallpox—the disease which killed or disfigured thousands until the advent of proper vaccination in the nineteenth century. She was lucky to survive and, despite the scars left by smallpox, 'she remained very agreeable. And being of a very civil and affable deportment . . . her company was loved and coveted by all who knew her.'[1] Several members of her family also dedicated themselves to the service of the Catholic Church—two of her brothers were Benedictine monks—and she herself died in 1676 after a lifetime of service. In the early days she had quietly persisted in her support of Father Baker and went from strength to strength. He left and went to England and the 1630s saw the provision of necessary buildings, not least a church, as well as a cemetery in 1637. Dame Catherine was abbess when the community was granted ownership in 1638 of the Cambrai buildings which had originally been loaned to it. By 1641 the community was promoted to the status of an abbey, with the independence that abbeys, unlike smaller establishments such as priories, enjoy. In 1655 Dame Catherine led the nuns politely to refuse to obey the demand of the President of the General Chapter of the English Benedictine Congregation to surrender to him all their books 'in order to purge the books' which he might deem likely to lead them to 'feed upon poisonous doctrine.' It is clear from this episode why she had been selected in 1641 to spend those four years reforming the nearby convent

1 Dame Laurentia McLachlan, *Stanbrook Abbey; A Sketch of its History* (Burns, Oates and Washbourne, 1925) pp. 16–17.

of French nuns and how, despite her quiet and self-effacing manner, she was a force to be reckoned with. Unfortunately, during her absence standards appear to have slipped at home with, instead of the prescribed silence, too much chattering in the refectory and, at divine service, late arrivals who 'laugh and whisper one to another . . . for want of preparing their bookes.' Abbess Christina, in office 1641–45, also complained that some nuns 'speake verie sharply' and showed 'verie disgustfull looks and dislikes,' observing that such faults were 'not our former custome.'[1]

The community of nuns, originally called that of Our Lady of Comfort, was renamed that of Our Lady of Consolation of the Order of St Bennet (Benedict). Our Lady—Mary, mother of Christ—was widely revered and regarded as a source of comfort or consolation at that time, especially in mainland Europe. Although for many years the community had financial problems, by the eighteenth century it was commonly known as 'Paradise'. This implies a comfortable lifestyle which was not the reality, particularly in the cash-strapped years of the mid-seventeenth century. Daily life followed a Benedictine pattern adapted to need: rising at 6 a.m., the nuns attended prime, terce, sext and none before dinner at 11 a.m. In the afternoon and evening they went to vespers and compline before retiring to bed at 8 p.m., their sleep interrupted by matins and lauds at midnight. There were also frequent masses to attend. Time between services was devoted to various practical and religious tasks.

> [Life] included strict canonical enclosure, the regular practice of mental prayer and spiritual reading . . . and the celebration of the Divine Office with a good deal of choral solemnity: all calculated

1 Heather Wolfe, *Cambrai's Imprint on the Life of Lady Falkland* (paper given in 1998 at the English Benedictine Congregation History Commission Symposium) pp. 7–8.

> to instil that great care and devotion in regard to points of monastic observance which have marked the community ever since.[1]

Those hours spent each day in prayer, singing the offices (services) in their small chapel and practising silent contemplation meant that they were thus expected to stand, kneel or sit in a usually cold church for about five hours out of every twenty-four; some of that time was, of course, in the middle of the night. Monastic life, lived conscientiously, has never been for the faint-hearted.

Education and other intellectual pursuits were, from the earliest days, very highly rated at Cambrai. A small school was soon established, some of the pupils going on to become nuns.[2] In a policy which might be seen as a forerunner of their successful printing activity at Stanbrook, the nuns' scholarly activities involved writing, copying and translating religious manuscripts. These included medieval works such as those of Julian of Norwich, one of the earliest female writers on theology, who died about 1416. Practical work such as spinning and church embroidery was also important, as was, rather unexpectedly, cut-paper or cut-parchment craft, a prized specimen of which survived to be cherished at Stanbrook. Carried out in the community's simple brick buildings, such work enabled the nuns to scratch together some small income.[3] The people of Cambrai probably valued the English visitors the nuns attracted, while the women themselves, living in a manner so enclosed that few of them could speak any French, made no demands on the town.

The early Cambrai nuns particularly valued the support of the learned and pious Archbishop Francis Vanderburg, who had welcomed them into his diocese and had a special interest

1 Benedictines of Stanbrook, *In a Great Tradition* (John Murray, 1956) p. 21.

2 McLachlan, *Stanbrook Abbey,* pp. 20–21.

3 Lunn, *English Benedictines,* p. 174.

in the education of both girls and boys. He left their abbey £10 a year after he died at the age of seventy-seven in 1644. But the 1640s were a period of hardship for them as English Catholics at home in England, hard-pressed by the demands and tragedies of civil war between royalists and parliamentarians, were not able to give them the funds they needed to keep their community going. One very significant source of income had been the dowries from well-to-do families of young women wishing to enter monastic life, but this source had become much reduced in such troubled political and economic times. Continental Europe was also in turmoil, ravaged by the atrocities of the Thirty Years War from 1618 to 1648: like the English Civil War, this terrible war was caused by both political and religious differences. The Cambrai nuns, numbering fifty in 1645,[1] and struggling to support that number, were advised to disband but did not wish to become divided by entering numerous French religious houses. They decided to explore the possibility of setting up a house in Paris, which was the main destination in France for English Roman Catholic exiles. It was to Paris that the future Charles II fled, in order to see his mother, Henrietta Maria, soon after his defeat in September 1651 at Worcester, the final civil war battle. In November 1651 three nuns left Cambrai for Paris, together with a priest, five more following in February 1652. Bridget More, sister of their original spirited leader Dame Gertrude More, was in 1652 elected their first prioress, in office until 1665.

A New House in Paris

This small daughter house of the Cambrai community struggled along in rented accommodation in what came to be called the Left Bank area by the River Seine. Their numerous well-wishers included none less than Henrietta

1 Wolfe, *Cambrai's Imprint*, p. 6.

Maria, who had returned to her native France before the execution of her husband Charles I in 1649, but there was precious little money available to help them in those early days. Nevertheless, they left the rented, flood-threatened property when in 1664 they managed to buy a secluded house with a walled garden which became their home in the Champ de l'Alouette until the 1690s.

This Paris house, dedicated to Our Blessed Lady of Good Hope, did however receive a significant windfall as a result of a young nun, aged about fifteen, entering in 1665. She was Mary Appleby whose mother was by descent a Gascoigne—the family which had produced not only the remarkable Dame Catherine who served Cambrai so well and for so long as abbess, but also other distinguished religious leaders. Mary Appleby's mother had died when she and her sister were very young children and, some years after her father's remarriage, he was forced to honour a very generous settlement on the children of his first marriage, thus enabling her monastic home in Paris to benefit to the tune of £2500—a veritable fortune.[1] This small group of nuns remained in Paris for 130 years, was imprisoned in 1794 during the anti-clerical activities of the French Revolution and came to England in 1795.

It is not always recognised that two houses—the original one in Cambrai and the house in Paris—stemmed from the original little group set up in Cambrai in the 1620s and that both still survive. Whilst the Cambrai community came to Stanbrook and is now in Yorkshire, the Paris house, which became independent of Cambrai, survives in Colwich, Staffordshire. Their stories in the years following the French Revolution are remarkably similar. The Lady of

1 Arthur Bantoft, 'The Gascoigne Family and the Catholic Church in the 17th and 18th Centuries', *The Barwicker*, No. 69 (March 2003). Available at http://www.barwickinelmethistoricalsociety.com/6908.html

Good Hope nuns left Paris and stayed in London for a short time before going to Marnhill in Dorset. In 1807 they moved to Cannington in Somerset and then, in 1836, to Colwich, where their abbey, dedicated to St Mary, was modernised in the late twentieth century.[1] The story of the community of nuns that remained at Cambrai is the subject of the chapters which follow in this book.

1 Colwich Abbey website, http://www.colwichabbey.org.uk

CHAPTER TWO
Paradise Achieved—and Lost—in Cambrai

Building Paradise

About forty nuns had stayed in Cambrai during the hungry times of the seventeenth century, when money was short, and lived there, in peace, for another 150 years until the political upheaval and excesses of the French Revolution hit them in 1793. The fortunes of the abbey at Cambrai had much improved by the eighteenth century—how did this happen? Many of their documents having been lost during the events of the Revolution, details are not always clear but a key reason for this upturn in their fortunes lies with the generosity of affluent English families loyal to the old Catholic faith. It had always been the case that women from well-to-do families who became nuns brought with them dowries which helped to build considerable resources for their communities. There is evidence that, after the English constitutional upheavals of the seventeenth century, money once more started to flow in, as significant sums were brought to the abbey by new arrivals from wealthy families.[1] Whilst there was apparently no gift to Cambrai as valuable as the £2500 bestowed upon the Paris house, there were sizeable sums from the families of a number of nuns, many of whom were intelligent, well

1 Catholic Record Society, *Miscellanea*, vol. VIII (1913), pp. 48–85.

educated women bringing with them, too, intellectual accomplishments which at that time were the preserve only of wealthy people. Financial offerings included that brought by Elizabeth Kennet in 1697—£600 to build an infirmary and £100 for silver candlesticks for the church, as well as 'a plentiful portion.'[1] About the same time the Honorable Jane Widdrington, one-time maid of honour to Charles II's queen, Catherine of Braganza, entered the convent and gave £100 for building a chapel in the nuns' graveyard.[2] There were many more sums, large and small, given as a result of women bringing what in other circumstances might have been a marriage portion—which of course it was, since nuns are often said to be brides of Christ.

There were also gifts such as those mentioned in 1667 made by Paul Robinson:

> Who had obliged this Convent by many Donations given at several times in rents and ready money, to the value of more than £500 sterling, besides the very many more friendly offices of great importance for which he deserves to be gratefully remembered by us.[3]

To help put into economic context the level of generosity shown in gifts such as these, we might note that Sir Thomas Gascoigne 'our good Benefactor' who gave generously in several ways, settled £10 each yearly on his daughter and niece, which may be an indication that such a sum would maintain a nun. His son, also Sir Thomas, who had already given numerous 'considerable Alms to us,' left £200 to the Cambrai convent when he died in 1698. As the surviving Cambrai records state, 'our Convent has great obligations to that Family, who from

1 Ibid., pp. 58.
2 Ibid., pp. 59.
3 Ibid., pp. 82.

first beginning have been good Benefactors to us.'[1]

Life in the Cambrai house was, by the mid-eighteenth century, truly a place which lived up to the name by which it was commonly known, Paradise, and was a powerful magnet for young women like the Partington sisters, Mary and Elizabeth. Their Lancashire home was close to Preston where Catholics were harassed and persecuted mercilessly by people keen to earn the large reward of £100 for reporting the whereabouts of priests.[2] The younger girl, Mary, went first to Cambrai at the age of seventeen in 1768 and Elizabeth went in 1773 at the age of twenty-nine. She took the name of Ann Teresa and her various writings about the events of the latter part of the eighteenth century are invaluable. She produced an inventory of Paradise from which, in the 1950s, Dame Felicitas Corrigan was able to illustrate the joys of the Cambrai accommodation after all those early years of struggle, adding a wry comment on how different was her own experience of life at Stanbrook in the mid-twentieth century:

> [At Cambrai the] wainscotted church was paved with marble, [there was an organ of high quality] valued at £200 sterling, vestments of gold and silver tissue, the library stocked with a thousand books. [The refectory had] its black and white marble floor and handsomely carved pulpit. [There were] dormitories, the twenty-eight cells for the nuns and the six bedrooms containing 'two beds in each and decently furnished' in the infirmary quarters, together with other appurtenances which to the Stanbrook of today strike a note of positive luxury. The infirmary was provided with its own dining-room and still-room, the latter complete with 'a large herbal book, forty-two good copper stills, and every necessary utensil for Stilling and Medcinings', while

1 Ibid., p. 83.
2 Benedictines of Stanbrook, *In a Great Tradition* (John Murray, 1956) p. 31.

the chapter house was half-wainscotted, with a handsomely inlaid floor, and contained an altar supported on two pillars which was an object of evident pride.[1]

The French Revolution

After living for twenty years in this paradise, Dame Ann Teresa's world, like that of other religious, fell catastrophically apart. During the vicious years of the French Revolution religion was proscribed. The inmates of monasteries and nunneries became obvious targets of persecution by the revolutionaries—strong in Cambrai—who frequently visited the nearby nuns. We have painful yet fascinating detail about this period because Dame Ann Teresa, who died in England in 1820 in her mid-seventies, wrote an account of the terrifying experience which she had endured in middle age. In 1793 Cambrai was preparing for a siege. On Sunday 13 October four Commissioners arrived at the convent at 8.30 p.m., when the sisters were in bed, to tell them that everything they owned was now the property of the nation of which they were now prisoners to be kept under strict guard. The two priests acting as their confessors, one of them, Father Walker, very elderly and frail, were taken away as prisoners, leaving the nuns in fear that the men would be executed. In fact, despite being starved, they survived and were later sent to the same prison in Compiègne as the nuns, who on Friday 18 October were sent from Cambrai to this dreadful place of detention.

On that terrible Friday more soldiers came. They told the nuns, who had hoped and been led to believe that they would be allowed to stay in their home at Cambrai, that they must leave it within minutes. Each was allowed to take with her only a small bundle. Surprised and 'stupefied with grief,'[2] some left with nothing but the clothes they were wearing which were,

1 Ibid., p. 32

2 Catholic Record Society, *Miscellanea*, vol. VIII, p. 22. Ann Theresa Partington's account as transcribed.

unfortunately, the habits of their religious order which had been declared by the revolutionary government to be illegal attire. Fifteen professed nuns, five lay sisters and one novice were taken under escort to Compiègne via Bapaume, Peronne, Ham and Noyon. The fact of their being in open carts enabled the inhabitants of the towns through which they passed to see their illegal dress, though some of the soldiers were humane enough to lend them their cloaks 'to keep them from starving.'[1] They were still, however, open to the particularly strong abuse reserved for anyone showing allegiance to the church and, although the distance from Cambrai to Compiègne—about sixty miles on modern roads—could now be covered easily in an hour or two, those open carts on poor eighteenth-century roads took five painful days. They were given very little food – indeed some of the nuns had nothing to eat for two days. Their overnight accommodation was so basic that when they reached Ham they were relieved that the Governor, described in the account as a 'humane man', ordered that they were to be given a room to themselves and 'clean straw which was spread all over the floor. They were happy to lye down upon it, and the night passed without any noise of interruption.' In Noyon the next day the populace threatened to kill them and cheered the horse that kicked a particularly exhausted nun who, 'scarcely able to stand', had fallen at its feet.

At last they reached Compiègne, where they were thrown into a former convent infirmary, converted to use as a prison. Fed very basic but adequate food, they huddled together in a cold room in constant fear of being guillotined during the fearsome Reign of Terror. Most of them survived that winter, though in January and February a few died from some kind of jail fever, as did their elderly confessor, Father Walker. On 11 March 1794 the nuns were told that, since they had not paid for

1 Ibid. In this context *starving* means becoming very cold.

the food they had been given in the last few months, they would in future have nothing but coarse brown bread and water. It was clearly futile to explain to their captors that they had no money or property because it had all been confiscated by revolutionary soldiers. A plea from a local surgeon that a little broth be given to a nun who was aged nearly eighty and had been confined to bed with a fever for six weeks was refused. The nuns' efforts to raise a little money by taking in needlework for local people yielded, as might be expected, next to nothing. Only the charity of a well-wisher enabled each of them to keep her mattress and one blanket, which they had been told were to be taken away and replaced by 'a few locks of straw.'[1] Particularly intimidating behaviour by their guards in May 1794 and mention of the word *guillotine* by one commanding officer added to their fear that they were to be guillotined. At this time their simple beds were searched and anything of the smallest value, such as a small thimble used for their needlework, was confiscated.

In June 1794 a local community of sixteen Carmelite nuns from Compiègne was brought to the prison, but no communication was allowed between the Benedictines of Cambrai and the Carmelites. About a month later, on 16 July, these Carmelites, aged between thirty and seventy-nine, were taken to Paris and guillotined during the frenzy of executions of that summer. Their sad story has been told in works such as Gertrud von le Fort's 1933 novel *A Song at the Scaffold* and in William Bush's 1999 history *To Quell the Terror*, celebrating their courage as on the way to the scaffold they sang the Litany of the Blessed Virgin. Although not allowed to speak to each other, the Carmelite nuns waved to the Cambrai nuns as they left for their final journey to Paris. The Mayor of Compiègne was as helpful to the Cambrai Benedictine nuns as he could dare to be: in an effort to get them clothes which would make them less conspicuous targets for anti-religious

1 Ibid., p. 28

For over two hundred years the Benedictine nuns of Stanbrook have treasured the relics of the Carmelite nuns who were thrown into prison with them at Compiègne. After the Carmelites were guillotined, showing great courage as they were carted away in their monastic dress, some of their secular clothes, shown here, were given to the Benedictines and brought to England. *Photographs courtesy of Stanbrook Abbey.*

fanatics, he had sent to them the secular clothing left behind by the Carmelites who had been beheaded in their religious clothing These very ordinary clothes, poor though they were, came to be held in great reverence by the Benedictine community. In the early twentieth century, on the pope's authority, the clothes were recognised as holy relics of martyrs who had died for their faith and were beatified in 1906.

The Cambrai nuns' continuing fear that they, too, would be sent to the guillotine was reinforced by the blunt remark of a jailer that the shoes which they lacked and which the Mayor promised to get for them would not be required for long. Their fears were well-founded: in France the period from June 1793 until July 1794 became infamous as the Reign of Terror, masterminded by Maximilien Robespierre, a leading member of the so-called Committee of Public Safety. Countless men and women were killed: some claim that ten thousand people died in prison and seventeen thousand were sent to the guillotine because they were perceived as public enemies by Robespierre and his fellow revolutionaries.[1] The days of Robespierre were, however, numbered: he was guillotined at the end of July 1794, nearly two weeks after the Carmelites were killed, and his fearful regime was over.

With the mass beheadings coming to an end the Cambrai nuns were spared the horrors of the guillotine and managed to survive the very severe 1794–95 winter despite insufficient food, clothing and fuel in the bitterly cold prison. They were also given rather more freedom of movement. In truth, life outside the prison was scarcely any better than that inside: the new authorities in France could put neither food into hungry mouths nor fuel and clothing where they were sorely needed. Life was barely supportable as France tore itself apart, and English people trapped in the country started to make ever more strenuous efforts to get back to England.

1 http://www.britannica.com/event/Reign-of-Terror

Encouraged by the mayor, the nuns sought passports to England, with little hope that they would be granted. To their indescribable relief, the abbess and three older nuns were allowed on 24 April 1795 to leave for Calais, the rest following a few days later in two carts. Passing sadly past their old home in Cambrai, which had been turned into a prison, they reached Calais and in the evening of Sunday 2 May they landed at Dover. The next day they went by coach to Charing Cross, London. Remarkably, of the twenty-one who left Cambrai, seventeen had survived.

Safety in England

The obvious—and not easily answered—question is why the Cambrai community (like the community in Paris which eventually went to Colwich) were spared in a France which had turned so vehemently against those who practised and fostered Catholicism. The religion had for centuries been widely supported, albeit with reservations that had rumbled on for generations after the religious upheavals of the protestant reformation in Europe. The fact that the nuns were English immigrants cannot be an entirely satisfactory explanation, particularly since the French under Napoleon would soon be planning the invasion of Britain. Violent revolution is, however, rarely either efficient or logical, and foreigners present particular problems. The Cambrai nuns were in the end able to make contact with quite well-to-do people in England, particularly Edward Constable of Burton, nephew of one of the community. He had in the past promised financial help, and delivered it willingly and promptly when it was needed for the sisters to make their way to England.

Whatever the answer, the prayer that Dame Gertrude More had written in the seventeenth century seems apposite:

> Thou hast shewed so much Providence towards this house, that if we cast not our whole care both for body and soul upon Thee, we shall not deserve the favours Thou hast shewed to us. We are Thy

little flock; keep Thou ever possession of us; let us be of one mind and one heart; Thou hast called us and gathered us together; send us a good life and a happy death to Thy praise, honour and glory, who art God of all things, and to whom now and for ever be given all laud and praise by all creatures. Amen. Amen.

Such money as the community possessed had remained in France, and it was decided by the protective Benedictine authorities that the Cambrai nuns should go to Woolton, near Liverpool, where a Benedictine monk, Dom Bede Brewer, ran a small mission. Having responsibility for a school, he planned to hand this over to the Cambrai refugees. Exhausted after their journey from France, but somewhat rested after over two weeks in London, where they 'received every civility and kindness,'[1] the nuns were disappointed when they reached their new home to find that there was no chapel. Wearing the monastic habit was not at this time allowed in England and, worst of all, they could not celebrate Mass until a French priest, Abbé Pernéz, was provided at the expense of Edward Constable, who had already given them so much. Constable also made the community an annual allowance of £60.

Prematurely aged by their experience in Compiègne, some nuns never completely recovered. As Dame Felicitas Corrigan wrote eleven years after the horrors of Nazi concentration camps had been revealed in 1945, one could truthfully say that Compiègne was no Auschwitz or Belsen. Even at the worst time of the nuns' imprisonment they were never physically assaulted. But Dame Agnes Robinson, a thirty year old nun who, because she was able to speak French, 'bore the brunt of the interrogations, trembled from head to foot for the rest of her life.'[2]

1 Catholic Record Society, *Miscellanea*, vol. VIII, p. 22. Ann Theresa Partington's account as transcribed.

2 Benedictines of Stanbrook, *Great Tradition*, p. 40

Salford Hall, where the community lived for thirty years before acquiring the Stanbrook estate in the 1830s. *Image courtesy of Stanbrook Abbey.*

Until 1802 they were led by Abbess Lucy Blyde, who had been appointed less than a year before their arrest in 1793 and bore the heavy weight of leadership during their imprisonment and their disappointments and re-adjustment at Woolton. Four of the nuns died at Woolton and were buried in nearby Childwall churchyard.[1] They scraped a living by teaching five- to fifteen-year-old year old girls a curriculum which included French, English, geography, arithmetic and religious education. Each was also granted a small monthly pension by the government.

They stayed at Woolton for about twelve years, until Mr Constable asked Mrs Stanford, owner of Salford Hall in Abbots Salford in Warwickshire, to allow them to stay there at a rent they could afford. Mrs Stanford obtained the consent of her heir-at- law, Mr Berkeley of Spetchley. She also paid £100 towards their removal expenses when in 1807 they moved south to Salford, where they continued to run a school to help

1 Gateacre Society Records (2006).

with expenses. By 1826 the long cherished hope of a return to Cambrai was abandoned: their beautiful abbey was ruined after being used as a prison. About a thousand valuable books and many irreplaceable original manuscripts, seized by the revolutionaries from their Paradise, were damaged by storage in damp accommodation. A few years later, together with items taken from other monasteries, some were to form part of the collection housed in the newly founded Cambrai museum. Nearly a hundred years later almost all were to be lost when the Hotel de Ville at Cambrai was burned down during the devastation of the First World War.[1] Fortunately some survived and copies had been made of many others: some had been held by the Paris house and eventually went to Colwich.

The community stayed at Salford until a more permanent and suitable home in England could be found. The last of the Cambrai nuns died in 1830 at Salford Hall and in the 1830s, after nearly forty years of uncertainty, the community found its new home. Salford Hall is now a hotel and—perhaps inevitably—lays claim to the ghost of a nun!

1 Wolfe, *Cambrai's Imprint*, p. 4.

CHAPTER THREE
At Home in Stanbrook

Stanbrook Hall

The nuns' new home was Stanbrook Hall; the name Stanbrook dates back to the thirteenth century[1] and probably means stony marshland. In 1755 Alderman Richard Case of Worcester had bought a few acres of land with two tenements in Stanbrook End, Powick, near Worcester and built the Hall in the latter part of the eighteenth century. In 1797, when the nuns were struggling at Woolton, Stanbrook Hall was put up for sale and described as follows:

> All that capital and Substantially Built Freehold Mansion and Premises, called Stanbrook Hall, of which immediate possession will be given, situate on a pleasing eminence in the delightful and healthy Village of Powick, three miles from the City of Worcester, commanding delightful as well as extensive views over a rich and most fertile Country, within one mile of the Severn, and five miles distant only from the Malvern Hills, and in a country which may truly be called the Garden of England.
>
> These premises forming a most desirable residence for a Family of respectability and fortune, have spacious and very lofty sitting and eating Rooms. The Library and Breakfast Room 21 feet by

1 A. Mawer, F. M. Stenton and F. T. S. Houghton, *The Place-Names of Worcestershire* (C.U.P., 1969) p. 226.

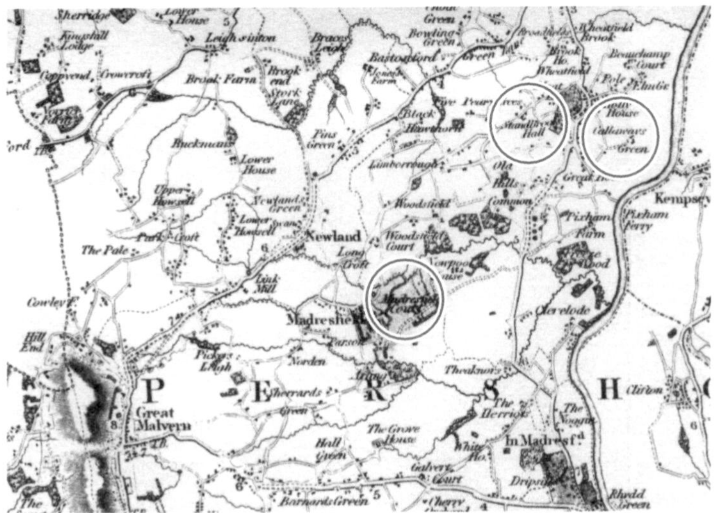

Part of Christopher Greenwood's 1822 map of Worcestershire, showing Madresfield Court (centre) and Standbrook Hall marked to the left of Callaways Green (Callow End).

> 18 feet. The Drawing Room, 24 feet by 18 feet, and the Eating Parlour, 21 feet by 18 feet, and 15 feet in height, handsomely fitted up with Marble Chimney pieces etc.
>
> Numerous bedchambers, with attached Dressing Rooms, two excellent Staircases . . . various suitable Domestic Offices, Coach House and Granary, Dove Cote and stews for the preservation of Fish, and comprising in the whole, including Garden and Orchard, about 33 acres of most admirable Land.[1]

Embellished and extended, this estate was sold in 1818 to Abraham Thompson, who went to the West Indies soon after his purchase. He decided in 1835, after his return to England, to sell the estate. The nuns were very keen to purchase it but were well aware of the prejudice which was still prevalent against all things Roman Catholic despite the Catholic Emancipation Act of 1829, giving Catholics full civil liberties. A little subterfuge

1 McLachlan, *Stanbrook Abbey*, p. 59.

(Left) Stanbrook Hall in 1835 a year before its purchase by the community. *Image courtesy of Stanbrook Abbey and Michael Hill.*

(Right) During the two years after its purchase in 1836, old Stanbrook Hall was adapted and extended for occupation by the nuns. The work by architect Charles Day was sympathetic to the existing Georgian buildings towards the left and included a newly built chapel on the right, as well as a refectory, some cells and a chapter-room for meetings, so named because in medieval times chapters from the Rule of St Benedict would have been read aloud there. *Image courtesy of Stanbrook Abbey.*

was practised by their friend, Dom Bernard Short, who was in charge of a mission in Little Malvern. Setting aside his clerical clothing, 'a handsome man with courteous manners, and well fitted to play the part of a country gentleman'[1] he rode over in a bottle-green coat, wearing boots and spurs, to inspect the estate, being careful to ask about local provision for shooting and hunting as well as the cellarage for wine, an enquiry which enabled him to check how dry the basements were. The sale was completed on 18 November 1836, Mr Thompson's anger at having sold his estate for the purpose of its being turned into a Roman Catholic nunnery coming too late for the deed to be undone.

The buildings needed both repairs and extension. Although the nuns could not therefore settle in properly for two years, they started work on the land, hiring a man to plough it before November was out. During the ensuing months the Georgian buildings were repaired, and a new chapel, chapter room, refectory and cells, as well as a separate school building, were

1 Ibid., p. 58

Taken about 1900, this picture shows the inside of Charles Day's chapel after it had been adapted for use as the chapter house. *Photograph courtesy of Stanbrook Abbey and Michael Hill.*

erected using the plans of the County Surveyor, Charles Day, who also designed Worcester's Shire Hall in the mid-1830s.A curious episode occurred on 27 April 1838, about a month before the nuns moved into Stanbrook. Under the supervision of the indomitable Sister Mary Ann McArdle men dug up eight bodies from the Salford burial ground. Included among the 'relics of their dear departed sisters' were those of two who had endured the hardships of imprisonment at Compiègne and also of one who had died since the purchase of Stanbrook and was buried in a very shallow grave to facilitate removal. With the utmost secrecy these bodies were carted off to be buried in a graveyard at the new monastery in Stanbrook. A particular difficulty arose over the body of Dom Augustine Lawson, their beloved spiritual leader, who had been put into a very heavy lead-lined wooden coffin which—unfortunately and very obviously—weighed down the lightly sprung cart on to which it was loaded! Despite the curiosity of a toll-house keeper on the turnpike road to Stanbrook, the illegal transport of the bodies was achieved and they were safely re-interred in the old mortuary at Stanbrook.[1] As Dame Felicitas Corrigan commented, 'in actual truth it was our dead who took possession of the monastery in our name.'

Conscious of prejudice against their religion and their perceived intrusion into the area, the nuns nevertheless found that they had some local friends such as the third Earl Beauchamp of Madresfield Court, so kindly to his tenants that he earned the nickname 'the peasants' earl.' To have such an influential landowner in the district on their side was of considerable importance to them: his kindness to the nuns enabled them to secure a diversion to a footpath which threatened the privacy required by a contemplative order. That privacy was later reinforced and permanently secured by the erection in the 1870s of a fine brick wall, which still stands as a remarkable feature of Callow End and of the work of the later Pugins.

Could the Abbey Survive?

Life at Stanbrook started modestly. In small chaises and pony carriages, the nuns arrived at their new home in the spring of 1838 having visited Benedictine houses *en route* in places such as Coughton, Redditch and Worcester. Given their normal seclusion they would have found this journey highly stimulating, and their eventual arrival at Stanbrook, a realisation of their long cherished dreams, was an exciting new beginning. Removal from Salford Hall was completed by 21 June and their first Mass at Stanbrook was celebrated on Sunday 15 July 1838. Their Chaplain in the early 1840s was Dom Luke Barber, who became President of the English Benedictine Congregation but lived at Stanbrook until his death in 1850. He took great care of their interests, seeking to improve the property by further purchases, such as an old

1 Benedictines of Stanbrook, *Great Tradition*, p. 54

W. H. Wood's idyllic 1868 portrayal of nuns in front of the west side of the chapel with children, presumably pupils at the abbey's school, playing decorously on the lawn. *Image courtesy of Stanbrook Abbey and Michael Hill.*

blacksmith's shop, on the site of which new stables and a lodge were built.[1] But some of the nuns were deeply disappointed that they were still not able to resume the enclosed, contemplative life that their order had originally led during the years in Cambrai. The rituals and liturgy were also a pale shadow of what earlier generations practised. The necessity for the community to develop a school as a means of livelihood meant that the original aims of the foundation had been sacrificed to such an extent that ten years after their arrival at Stanbrook their old friend and new chaplain, Dom Bernard Short, felt moved to say in the mid-1840s to a potential novice, 'This is hardly a religious house, you know, but just a pious, happy little family.'[2] This was a few years after a visit to Rome during which the Italian Cardinal

1 McLachlan, *Stanbrook Abbey*, pp. 63–64

2 Dame Eanswythe Edwards, 'The Influence on the English Benedictine Congregation of Dom Gueranger's Revival.' A paper given in 1975 at the English Benedictine Congregation History Commission Symposium.

Another of W. H. Wood's 1868 watercolours showing visitors to Stanbrook Hall. Wood's pictures seem to reinforce the view that the community at this time was just 'a pious happy family'. *Image courtesy of Stanbrook Abbey and Michael Hill.*

Alessandro Barnabo had bluntly said to him, 'as for Stanbrook, the best thing we can do is just to let it quietly die out.'[1]

Dom Bernard suffered from poor health and in 1863 Dom Laurence Shepherd, a cheerful and earnest man, said to 'live for the holy liturgy,'[2] became the Stanbrook chaplain who 'laboured in re-establishing the choral solemnities of chant and ceremonial.'[3] Experience at Ampleforth and Bath in England, at Parma in Italy and, especially, at the newly revived abbey of Solesmes in France's beautiful Loire Valley had all given him a deep knowledge of monasticism and liturgy together with a desire to spread that knowledge. He and Abbess Scholastica Gregson, 'a woman of consummate virtue,'[4] who was abbess from 1846 until 1862 and from 1868 to 1872, worked at restoring the foundations of monastic

1 Ibid.

2 McLachlan, *Stanbrook Abbey*, p. 66

3 Ibid. p. 67

4 Benedictines of Stanbrook, *Great Tradition*, p. 55

The nuns' original burial ground is portrayed somewhat flamboyantly by W. H. Wood in 1868. *Image courtesy of Stanbrook Abbey and Michael Hill.*

life at Stanbrook. The state of things may be deduced by the response to a request by Dame Benedict Anstey in 1868 to see, before taking her vows, the Constitutions by which Stanbrook was regulated. She must have been shocked to hear the rather embarrassing reply of the abbess, 'to tell you the truth, there are none; perhaps something may be done later.'[1]

It was. Within weeks Father Laurence had researched the work of his mentor, Dom Guéranger, the first abbot and key figure in the growing fame of the French abbey which he had revived at Solesmes. In January 1869 he went to consult Guéranger and obtained his permission to introduce at Stanbrook Constitutions similar to those which Guéranger had devised for Solesmes. The Pope eventually confirmed them for Stanbrook. In addition to those new Constitutions, Father Laurence set about giving the community a thorough

1 Edwards, 'The Influence on the English Benedictine Congregation of Dom Gueranger's Revival.'

STANBOOK CONVENT,

Near Worcester.

THE BENEDICTINE COMMUNITY,

ORIGINALLY

ESTABLISHED AT CAMBRAY,

Continue to receive YOUNG LADIES, upon the following Terms:

For BOARD, WASHING, and EDUCATION (including French), THIRTY FIVE POUNDS Per Annum. –One Guinea Entrance.

The Italian Language, Music, Drawing, and Dancing, form *separate Charges.*

The Harp, ...

.. Piano, ...

.. Italian, ...

.. Drawing, ...

.. Dancing, ...

Each Young Lady is required to be provided with two Pair of Sheets, six Hand Towels, Knife and Fork, and a Silver Table and Tea Spoon.

A Uniform of Buff Calico is worn in the Summer, and a Dark Merino in the Winter; White on Sundays.

PAYMENT TO BE MADE HALF-YEARLY IN ADVANCE.

LEICESTER AND SON, PRINTERS, WORCESTER.

An advertisement *c.* 1840 for the Stanbrook Convent school. The Worcester printer omitted the capital *R* in the heading—an oversight of which the Stanbrook Abbey press, founded some years later, would have been unlikely to be guilty! *Image courtesy of Christine Bannister.*

knowledge of liturgy and a command of the Latin needed for understanding and interpreting it. He had learned the need for all this from studying the work of Guéranger, who worked tirelessly at Solesmes until his death in 1875. Against all odds in a France still recovering from revolution, Guéranger had revived Roman Catholic liturgy and Gregorian chant. Father Laurence yearned to do something similar at Stanbrook. With Abbess Scholastica, he recognised that, if it were to emulate Solesmes, Stanbrook needed to build a fine new church in which ritual, liturgy and music could be celebrated with maximum effect—an achievement which was not possible in Day's modest 1830s chapel.

Changing Attitudes in England

In the thirty years since the nuns had entered their new home in Stanbrook some change had taken place in attitudes to religion in England. Although John Rayer Lane, respected farmer of nearby Castlemorton, grumbled to his diary in 1866 that he feared 'greatly that Ritualism is gaining ground rapidly as the newspapers of the last week are full of descriptions of Church decorations and other tomfoolery leading to Romanism,'[1] it is also true that such open discussion suggests public interest and possibly a degree of sympathy greater than that prevailing in earlier times. The 1870 declaration of papal infallibility in matters of doctrine—a belief which non-Catholics found, and often still find, incomprehensible—may have caused a hiccup in the process of developing fraternity between different forms of Christianity. Nevertheless, Roman Catholic dioceses were being developed and the old fears of Roman Catholics as less than patriotic were on the wane.

Times were changing and Stanbrook Abbey was about to make its mark. After the high standards and contemplative

1 Pamela Hurle, *Castlemorton Farmer; John Rayer Lane 1798–1871* (Pamela Hurle, 1996) p. 59.

life at Cambrai had been shattered by the French Revolution in the 1790s, the hope of re-establishing them in France had been dashed by the 1830s. Father Laurence could see the possibility of reviving them in England: Paradise, lost for ever in France, might yet be re-created in England.

Nuns in the garden at Stanbrook Hall. *Photograph courtesy of Stanbrook Abbey and Michael Hill.*

CHAPTER FOUR
Change, Expansion and Growing Confidence

Impact of the Oxford Movement in the Church of England

In the 1830s the Oxford Movement encouraged re-thinking on the nature of worship within the Church of England, the established church of the country. Young Oxford theologians, favouring a return to some of the ritual which had prevailed in the medieval period of the church's greatest influence, hoped that it would revive the flagging influence of the established church and offer some challenge to the more emotional appeal of nonconformity, with its Wesleyan hymns, stirring tunes and energetic preaching. Of course, during the medieval period the whole of Western Europe was Roman Catholic, so the revival of ritual smacked to many a nineteenth century member of the Church of England of a return to Catholic practices. This they found not only distasteful to their sense of how religious services should be conducted but also a threat to society and to the state because of the old fear of the papacy as a foreign influence. It is also worth remembering that this 1830s revival of ritual in the Church of England followed close on the heels of the 1829 Catholic Emancipation Act: there were those who thought things were looking suspiciously like a Roman Catholic resurgence which they did not welcome.

Although the Roman Catholic Church did gain some

converts, the Oxford Movement heralded the return of ritual to the Church of England and a revival of interest in religious debate. Interesting variations developed between so-called High Church, emphasising ritual, and Low Church, often quite close to the non-Conformist forms of service. Those churches which were strong supporters of the revival of medieval ritual became known as Anglo-Catholic. This revival was expressed physically in architectural features, commonly referred to as neo-Gothic, and also included a renewed respect for the chancel and altar area. Pointed arches appeared in windows and doorways, and intricate carving, stained glass and ornate wrought-iron work all contributed to the decline of the somewhat austere classical styles which had been popular in the eighteenth century. Spires re-appeared and box pews, which hid all kinds of inappropriate behaviour, gave way to the typically Victorian choir stalls and pews with notoriously uncomfortable backs. The gallery musicians, so well portrayed by Thomas Hardy, were made redundant by the installation of organs of varying quality—and of organists of similarly varied levels of competence. Victorian churches became more cluttered and more difficult to keep clean—like Victorian drawing rooms. For, indeed, the building of large numbers of new Anglican churches in neo-Gothic style soon re-invigorated much more than the building of places of worship for members of the established Church of England. The revival of Gothic styles of the medieval period was undoubtedly linked to religious doctrine, but the proliferation of domestic and public buildings—including protestant non-Conformist chapels—with Gothic features indicates that architects and their clients chose to imitate ecclesiastical features in secular building.

It is also true that the Roman Catholic Church won some interesting converts at this time. One of them was John

Henry Newman, who had been a leading figure in the Oxford Movement. After years of sometimes agonised thought he became a Roman Catholic, rose to be a cardinal and in 2010 was beatified by Pope Benedict XVI, opening the possibility of future canonisation. Augustus Welby Northmore Pugin was another influential convert whose architectural gifts and extraordinary energy meant that his impact was particularly widespread. He worked frenetically throughout his short life to encourage the revival of the medieval Gothic style of architecture, dying at the young age of forty in 1852.

Edward Welby Pugin

A. W. N. Pugin bequeathed to his son, Edward Welby Pugin, a passion and skills which are still evident even in what remains of Stanbrook's chapel, which the younger Pugin designed in 1869, six years before his death at the age of forty-one. Like his father, he died young, his death following a period of hard work probably exacerbated by his rather belligerent and litigious nature, which proved financially unfortunate. Whatever his problems, he made his name by designing churches and chapels for Roman Catholics—like those at Stanbrook—who were very gradually finding life more comfortable as prejudice against them became less pronounced.

At Stanbrook his discussions with Father Laurence Shepherd led to modifications in his design of its church—particularly to the bell-tower: indeed the priest climbed 'fearlessly past the scaffolding and up the turret to . . . set a cross at the tower's summit.'[1] Consecrated in 1871 by William Bernard Ullathorne, first Roman Catholic Bishop of Birmingham, the abbey church initially consisted of chancel, nave and one transept chapel, another transept chapel—that of the Holy Thorn—being added in 1885. The whole edifice was a stunning example of

1 Stanbrook Abbey website: http://www.stanbrookabbey.org.uk

The design of the tower of the new church was influenced by Father Laurence Shepherd. The Worcester photographer Thomas Bennett took this picture before the new monastery accommodation was built. *Photograph courtesy of Stanbrook Abbey and Michael Hill.*

A modern picture showing the tower in sunlight. *Photograph courtesy of Andrew Grant and Neil Styles.*

Thomas Bennett's photograph, looking east, shows the elaborate interior of the church in 1871. Note the separation of the sanctuary from the choir by the decorative screen, removed in the late twentieth century. *Photograph courtesy of Stanbrook Abbey and Michael Hill.*

neo-Gothic style, containing what the outspoken Bishop Ullathorne later described, despite some misgivings as to the reforms at Stanbrook in the 1870s,[1] as the most beautiful sanctuary in his diocese.[2] The sanctuary was separated from the choir by a screen of fine wrought iron, emphasising in true Gothic manner the honour and sanctity of the altar. The

1 Judith Champ, 'William Ullathorne'. Paper given in 1985 at the English Benedictine Congregation History Commission Symposium.

2 Benedictines of Stanbrook, *Great Tradition*, p. 58.

This early twenty-first century view, also looking east, reflects change in the nature of worshipping practice. The elaborate screen—and much else—has disappeared. The high quality of materials and workmanship in the church and elsewhere is, however, still very apparent. *Photograph courtesy of Andrew Grant and Neil Styles.*

choir of the church, the acoustics and the attention to fine materials and expert workmanship at last gave the community its longed for opportunity to produce beautiful liturgical music in the heart of its home. Edward Welby Pugin had produced a masterpiece but, to the horror of the Pugin Society, some changes were made in the mid-twentieth century: the original high altar and reredos 'suffered mutilation in the late 1930s . . . and then [were] completely removed (together with J. Hardman Powell's metal screen) in 1971 when the Minton encaustic floor tiles in the chancel (designed by E. W. Pugin and J. H. Powell) were replaced by ones similar to those often found in public lavatories.'[1] Its current use as part of an hotel complex has necessitated further changes in the chapel, but its design and the quality of its embellishments, including

1 G. J. Hyland, 'Chronological Gazetteer of the Works of E. E. Pugin' http://www.thepuginsociety.co.uk/convent-chapels.html

Key figures in the expansion of the abbey were the architect E. W. Pugin and, shown here, Father Laurence Shepherd, who died in 1885, and Dame Gertrude d'Aurillac Dubois, who was abbess from 1872 until her death in 1897. When Father Laurence became chaplain at Stanbrook in 1863 he inspired the community to work at reintroducing liturgy of the highest standard into monastic life. Both were buried in fine tombs in the Chapel of the Holy Thorn. *Photographs courtesy of Stanbrook Abbey.*

New Zealand satinwood choir stalls and the kauri pine organ case on the north wall, remain impressive.[1] For the use of the priests needed to provide sacramental services, part of the old Stanbrook Hall was modified to form a Presbytery, linked by a corridor to the church.

In the 1870s, once the church was finished the next priority was to provide a purpose-built monastic complex, with living accommodation, domestic offices and all the necessary facilities for up to a hundred nuns to be properly enclosed but also to work to maintain themselves. E. W. Pugin produced plans[2] and Father Laurence had considerable input, as did the saintly Dom Hildebrand de Hemptinne who was to become in 1893 the leader of the English Benedictine Congregation. This body had an overview of monastic communities which, as the

1 http://www.britishlistedbuildings.co.uk/stanbrookabbey

2 Michael Hill Conservation Plan for Stanbrook Abbey (2005), p. 12.

Congregation traditionally encouraged, retained a good deal of independence. The input of Dame Gertrude d'Aurillac Dubois, who in 1872 succeeded Dame Scholastica Gregson as abbess, was also very significant. Father Laurence continued to be an enthusiastic champion, keen also to ensure that the new buildings included a good library. He bequeathed his own well stocked library to the nuns. Interested in printing, he also helped them to set up in 1876 the printing press which was to become world famous for the high quality of its books, illustrations and prints. Initially the plan was for the nuns to print material for use in their own community and in other Benedictine houses. Fittingly, one of their first undertakings was to print *The Holy Rule of St Benedict.* From modest beginnings with equipment costing less than £60, within seven years they built a three roomed printing department, and were beginning to be recognised for their commitment to high standards and an interest in a wider range of books with solid intellectual or religious value. They had much in common with businesses such as the Kelmscott Press, using hand-made paper and illustrations by talented calligraphers and artists.

In 1897 Abbess Gertrude was succeeded by Dame Cecilia Heywood, who was abbess for thirty-four years until 1931. *Photograph courtesy of Stanbrook Abbey.*

When E. W. Pugin died in 1875 Cuthbert and Peter Paul Pugin, his half-brothers, took over the architectural practice and implemented the plans, changed by father Laurence and de Hemptinne, for a new monastery.[1] The foundation stone was laid

1 See Michael Hill Conservation Plan for Stanbrook Abbey (2005), p. 15.

in 1878 and the distinctive building remains an architecturally important gem. This purpose built living accommodation was a major improvement for the nuns who had found living in the old Stanbrook Hall far from convenient. Importantly, the move enabled, at last, proper enclosure of the community. In 1880 the nuns moved into their compact and sparsely furnished new cells, each measuring from about twelve to seventeen metres square. Long corridors gave access to these cells, the design being a feature which acknowledged a desire for greater privacy than the old medieval style of monastic dormitories could provide. Even so, for many years each bathroom had to serve eight cells. In 1885 the Chapel of the Holy Thorn in memory of Father Laurence was built on the south side of the church and a further wing incorporating a refectory, common room and domestic offices was completed some years later. Other Pugin plans were never completed but the achievements in the last thirty years of the nineteenth century were transformative. Although the extensive buildings were never, in reality, as cosy inside as the warm red-brick construction might tempt one to expect, both the design and the building were of high quality.

Consolidation and Success

In 1897 Abbess Gertrude d'Aurillac Dubois died at the age of fifty-five after being 'struck down by an incurable malady,[1] having spent twenty-five years as a firm, decisive but kindly abbess. Daughter of a Huguenot family living in Berlin, after education by nuns in Brussels she had been sent by her widowed father to Stanbrook simply to perfect her English. Shocked by her decision to take monastic vows, he at first opposed but eventually accepted it. A born leader, she weathered the storm which ultimately led to the position of abbess becoming a perpetual appointment: this ended any element of uncertainty which had been caused in the past

1 McLachlan, *Stanbrook Abbey,* p. 71.

by the need to hold an election every four years. A most suitable wielder of abbatial authority during the exciting period when the extensive residential buildings were completed, she worked with Father Laurence towards what a twentieth-century Stanbrook nun called 'a new era in the history of Stanbrook.'[1] Abbess Gertrude's funeral, described in the Catholic publication *The Tablet* in the autumn of 1897, was attended by over forty Benedictine monks, who sang in the choir with fifty Stanbrook nuns. Many representatives, from Britain and abroad, of the English Benedictine Congregation also attended, including the Abbot of Solesmes, where Abbess Gertrude had spent nearly a year learning so much at the feet of Dom Guéranger about the newly formulated Constitutions of the Benedictines as well as the development of the liturgy. The Bishop of Birmingham remarked upon the 'vigorous spirit of monastic discipline and work which animates the community today. By that time there was suitable accommodation for the choir of fifty professed sisters . . . as well as for the lay sisters and the twenty-five young ladies of the school.' The eighteenth-century Paradise at Cambrai had not been recoverable, but Stanbrook had proved beyond all doubt its devotion and ability in the liturgical work of the monastic life. The bishop paid tribute to the musical life and work of Stanbrook in the 1890s:

> Nowhere can the chant of the church be heard to greater perfection than at Stanbrook Abbey—nowhere is the Divine Office performed with more dignity. The Lady Abbess taught by word and example that the opus Dei, the Liturgy of the Church, was the greatest and most important work that anyone could perform.'[2]

This was indeed a difference from the disparaging comments on Stanbrook made less than fifty years earlier.

1 Benedictines of Stanbrook, *Great Tradition*, p. 55.
2 *The Tablet* (30 October 1897) p. 38.

Abbess Gertrude's successor as abbess, Dame Cecilia Heywood, in her shy and somewhat self-effacing manner, concentrated on less spectacular but crucially important matters. Consolidating all that had been achieved since the catastrophe in France, her thirty-four years in office saw two unusual events. The first was correspondence with Carmelite nuns who had re-established a community at Compiègne after the horrors of the French Revolution. The clothes of their guillotined predecessors, worn by the Benedictine nuns of Cambrai on their desperate journey to England and always treated by them with great reverence, were officially recognised by papal authorities as holy relics of martyred women and placed in a gilded oak shrine in the Stanbrook chapel. The second event was the foundation in Brazil in 1911 of a religious house linked with Stanbrook. By 1925 it had thirty-five nuns and was the first of several houses founded on foreign soil.

At home in Stanbrook, Abbess Cecilia recognised that the community should give up its school, which had been established as a means of bringing in some money but which reduced the hours available for worship. She had herself been Mistress in charge of generations of young girls. One of these girls, fifteen-year-old Margaret McLachlan, had been received, weeping and reluctant, into the school in 1881 by Dame Cecilia. Margaret McLachlan took vows at Stanbrook and became Dame Laurentia. She unswervingly supported Abbess Cecilia as abbess and then, at the age of sixty-five, in poor health and reluctant as she had been fifty years earlier as a young girl, succeeded her in 1931 to become the revered and famous Abbess Laurentia McLachlan.

In quite a short period of about fifty years, Stanbrook Abbey had been transformed from, in those dismissive words of its chaplain, 'hardly a religious house . . . just a happy pious family' to a remarkably well-organised and competent religious house which was to continue in the twentieth century its pursuit of excellence in several spheres.

CHAPTER FIVE
Enclosed Nuns with Unenclosed Minds

Dame Laurentia McLachlan 1866–1953

After many years of exchanging long letters and engaging in lengthy discussions through the monastic grille, George Bernard Shaw wrote to his friend Dame Laurentia McLachlan, 'though you are an enclosed nun you do not have an enclosed mind, as so many women at large have.'[1] This says much about Shaw's opinion of women of his generation but says even more about the extraordinarily talented woman who became abbess of Stanbrook in 1931. After her election it is recorded that, a very active but sick sixty-five year old woman, she quietly slipped out to utter repeatedly at the sanctuary steps the simple prayer 'I can't. You must.'[2] She died in 1953, having spent nearly seventy of her eighty-seven years enclosed at Stanbrook: twenty-two of those years—a quarter of her life—she spent as abbess.

Born in January 1866 in Lanarkshire, Margaret McLachlan took the name Laurentia when she entered the Stanbrook community at the age of eighteen in 1884. Her interest in Gregorian chant had already been excited by a visit to the French abbey at Solesmes which had influenced Father Laurence Shepherd so deeply. Solesmes in the nineteenth century became

1 Felicitas Corrigan, *Friends of a Lifetime: Nun, the Infidel and the Superman* (Fount, 1990) p. 8.

2 Benedictines of Stanbrook, *Great Tradition*, p. 281.

Margaret McLachlan as a girl of eighteen. She became Dame Laurentia and in 1931 was elected Abbess of Stanbrook. *Photographs courtesy of Stanbrook Abbey.*

central to the revival and development of medieval plainsong, of which Gregorian chant, which had emerged in the sixth century soon after St Benedict produced his Rule, became the most popular form.

When Margaret McLachlan first came to Stanbrook's small school Father Laurence Shepherd was still working tirelessly on the revival of the liturgy and that work was bearing fruit. Her own interest in the subject continued unabated until by her forties she had become recognised at home and abroad as a leading authority on plainsong. As the mature Dame Laurentia, her role as Stanbrook's organist and choir-mistress provided the perfect opportunity to continue her researches, exchange views with other researchers and put into practice much of what she learned. Her scholarship and achievement in church music was recognised in 1934 when Pope Pius XI awarded her the *bene merenti* medal for services to the Catholic church. By then her duties as abbess, responsible for a community of eighty, coupled with increasing age and frailty, limited the time she could spend on her beloved musical interests.

But this warm and gifted woman managed to find time to develop friendships with many people, some famous. They included not only the devastatingly incisive George Bernard Shaw but also the pompous, self-satisfied Sidney Cockerell, curator of the Fitzwilliam Museum in Cambridge who famously claimed that he 'found it a pigsty and turned it into a palace.'[1] Hugh Whitemore's play *The Best of Friends*, based on the letters between the three characters, brings to life the extraordinary support, and sometimes chilly exchanges, between these two opinionated atheists and Dame Laurentia, a fierce, very able and cogent defender of her faith.

Dame Felicitas Corrigan 1908–2003

Much more detail on Abbess Laurentia and the history of the community is available in the work of Dame Felicitas Corrigan, another extremely talented and generous-spirited Stanbrook nun. Kathleen Corrigan, an English graduate, organ scholar and teacher, who took the name Felicitas, joined the community in 1933, two years after Dame Laurentia became abbess, and she later published a detailed record of the remarkable life and achievements of her mentor Abbess Laurentia. Entering monastic life at the age of twenty-five, Kathleen Corrigan had once thought the *News of the World* and a packet of cigarettes were more to her liking than the life of a nun. A diverse character, her outspoken manner and sense of humour could take people by surprise, as could her readiness to take control and her innate kindness. A superb organist, she also worked in Stanbrook's library, at its printing press, in the garden and at domestic duties. Furthermore, in much the same way as Abbess Laurentia, she

1 Wilfrid Blunt, *Cockerell* (Alfred A. Knopf, 1964) p. 135.

Nuns of enclosed contemplative orders such as that at Stanbrook talked with visitors through grilles like this until changes in the late twentieth century when grilles were removed. This picture of the guests' parlour was taken by Edward Ihnatowicz and dates from the mid-twentieth century. The word *parlour* is from the French word *parler* meaning to talk. *Photograph courtesy of Stanbrook Abbey.*

made time—and also had skill and energy enough—to become an acknowledged scholar and loyal friend to other talented men and women beyond the monastic grille. Like the older woman, Dame Felicitas was 'an enclosed nun with an unenclosed mind.' Gifted and intelligent, she greatly admired Helen Waddell, the medievalist whose writing included not only very scholarly work but also a highly acclaimed popular novel on the tragic love affair between Heloise and Peter Abelard, the proud and much admired twelfth-century theologian castrated through the spite of her jealous uncle. Corrigan's prize-winning biography of Waddell—readable and very detailed, despite their never actually meeting—exudes understanding and human warmth, giving her subject the recognition to which she is due and showing the nun's own claim to scholarship.

Other Friendships Through the Monastic Grille

Dame Felicitas enjoyed a long friendship with the sometimes prickly actor Alec Guinness, who wrote over eight hundred letters to her over forty years of that friendship after his conversion to Roman Catholicism in the 1950s.[1] His letters contain many references to their religion and his innermost thoughts, but both he and his wife wrote to this enclosed nun in a relaxed style about a wide range of topics, including complaints about some of their employees and about the punitive tax paid on his income. Guinness noted the difficulty that Dame Felicitas experienced in playing the organ because of rheumatism developing in her fingers and offered to pay for private treatment. By the time of her death it had become infinitely worse, doubtless exacerbated by living in buildings which, although very beautiful, were difficult and expensive to heat.

The mid-twentieth century was a period of considerable activity between Stanbrook Abbey and celebrities of the outside world. Iris Murdoch's visiting of a friend, a nun at Stanbrook, influenced her writing of perhaps her best known novel, *The Bell*, first published in 1958. The Irish soprano and harpist, Mary O'Hara, came to Stanbrook after the sad loss to Hodgkins disease of her young American husband, the poet Richard Selig, left her a very young widow. She took monastic vows in 1962 at the age of twenty-seven but left after twelve years, resuming her musical career and eventually marrying a former priest in 1985. Dame Felicitas also helped the once widely popular

1 Piers Paul Read, *Alec Guinness: The Authorised Biography* (Simon and Schuster, 2003).

writer Rumer Godden, who spent three years at Callow End, to acquire first hand understanding of the monastic life which found its way into her *In This House of Brede*, first published in 1969.

Siegfried Sassoon, whose powerful First World War poetry attracted great acclaim and, more recently, some controversy as to the significance of the slaughter, was an important author whose work was printed at Stanbrook. When the Abbey Press was about to print his *The Path to Peace* he held somewhat tense discussion with Dame Hildelith Cumming on the quality of the paper to be used and later wrote to Dame Felicitas—with whom he maintained correspondence from 1959 until his death in 1967—that he considered its publication in 1960 to be 'his coronation as a Catholic'.[1] An edition of five hundred copies on handmade paper with embellishments by the talented calligrapher and illustrator Margaret Adams, it has been rated as one of the finest publications by Stanbrook Press, produced in what may be called the golden age of the Press. This is reflected in the high price currently demanded for rare copies which are advertised for sale.

The Stanbrook Press

The Stanbrook Press which Dom Laurence Shepherd had set up in 1876 went through some difficult periods. In 1872, when Dame Scholastica Gregson resigned after a quarter of a century as abbess, her successor, thirty-year-old Dame Gertrude d'Aurillac Dubois, championed the printing press and thus presided over the birth of an unusual and successful enterprise which continued to flourish until the Second World War. By the 1950s there was declining interest in its work and the press was threatened with closure. Dame Hildelith Cumming, who as the abbey's cellarer from 1951–55 had responsibility for many of its

1 John Stuart Roberts, *Siegfried Sassoon* (Richard Cohen Books, 1999) pp. 322–23.

financial decisions, thought closure and the sale of the equipment to be the best way forward. Abbess Elizabeth Sumner, however, decided in 1955 to put her in charge of trying to revive the press! This she did with such consummate skill that it continued for the rest of the twentieth century, earning the distinction of becoming the oldest private press in the country with a high reputation for attention to detail, accuracy and beauty. She saw the importance of securing the work of artists such as Margaret Adams to embellish books published by the Stanbrook Press. Dame Hildelith herself was another of Stanbrook's outstanding nuns, who is always described by adjectives such as generous, enthusiastic and energetic in all the fields to which she devoted her eighty-two years. London-born in 1909 and brought up a Protestant, she was a very successful concert pianist whose musical gifts enabled her to make a significant contribution to the revival of liturgy after her conversion to Roman Catholicism and taking her monastic vows in 1946.

In the late twentieth century new developments in commercial book production—especially the rise of digital printing—effectively put an end to labour-intensive older methods such as the letter-press used by the nuns. Their printing equipment had to be sold by the time they moved to Wass in 2009. The years of highly praised printing work had, however, reinforced the cultural contribution which Stanbrook made in the twentieth century to the outside world as well as to the religious life. The intellectual and practical offerings of Stanbrook nuns made the community a very significant centre of excellence. It was home to the likes of Dame Hildelith with her music and printing, Dame Laurentia leading a revival of traditional plain chant in which she was seen as a world expert and Dame Felicitas with many well researched books to her credit. Intellectually robust, honest and perceptive, these were all persons of importance. None of these women or the women whom they influenced saw the contemplative monastic life as an escape from the world. Any community which can produce women of this calibre is, even if small in number, an impressive body of influence sending out ripples much further than might be expected from an enclosed group settled in an obscure Worcestershire hamlet.

A nun at her clothing ceremony is supported by the Community (background right). *Photograph courtesy of Stanbrook Abbey.*

CHAPTER SIX
Changes in the Roman Catholic Church and to Stanbrook

A Window Opened by Pope John XXIII

The Second Vatican Council, commonly known as Vatican II, was opened in October 1962 during the pontificate of Pope John XXIII, whose reign as a much loved pontiff lasted less than five years (1958–63). Often seen as the most significant event in the Roman Catholic Church during the twentieth century, the Council, which lasted until December 1965, sought to reform the church by making it more accessible. As Pope John opened a window he used this action as an analogy with what he wanted the Council to do: to open the windows of the church so that 'we can see out and the people can see in'. There may be some debate about the extent to which this was achieved—some would say too much and some too little. Undoubtedly, however, a most important reform was the revision of the liturgy, allowing services to take place in local languages throughout the world instead of the exclusive use of Latin which was often not understandable to congregations other than those in monastic communities like Stanbrook. The grilles, which the nineteenth-century Stanbrook nuns so desperately wanted in order to perpetuate the original intentions of the seventeenth-century nuns at Cambrai, were destined for removal and within half a century old practices were being questioned and sometimes abandoned.

By the time of Vatican II Stanbrook's charismatic Abbess

Laurentia had been dead for nine years. Her successor as the community's twenty-third abbess from 1953 until 1983 was Dame Elizabeth Sumner, born in South Africa in 1911. It was thus she who faced the challenges of uncertainty as to what Vatican II might decide and then had to address changes resulting from it in this country as well as at new and old communities in Brazil, Massachusetts and Uganda, which she supported and sometimes visited. Numbers of professed nuns had declined significantly from the record of eighty in 1934 when Dame Elizabeth first arrived at Stanbrook. Such a decline was attributable to numerous factors unrelated to her kindly rule and wise pragmatism during times of change not only within, but also outside of, the Catholic church. After the unprecedented devastation caused by the Second World War people had become more questioning, less willing to accept traditional teaching and, often, desirous of change in many spheres of activity. The past was well on the way to becoming a foreign country, as L. P. Hartley wrote in 1953 in the opening lines of *The Go-between*. Facts of change, which might or might not be progress, had to be faced.

Practical and Financial Considerations at Stanbrook

The buildings at Stanbrook, like many beautiful homes and estates, are very expensive to maintain. By the closing years of the twentieth century the struggle to maintain property with many financial and practical problems became an insupportable millstone for a small community of nuns, whose motivation was to lead a religious life: such responsibilities detracted from their ability to live the monastic life which was their *raison d'être*. This situation, together with declining numbers seeking the religious life, meant that harsh economic facts needed to be addressed. Whatever the degree of reluctance to leave Stanbrook, most accepted that more modest and more easily maintained accommodation must be found, using proceeds from the sale of

This aerial view of Stanbrook Abbey, Callow End, was taken in the afternoon sun and shows, across the cloister garth, the shadow of the tower of the church which dominated life in the enclosed contemplative community for over a century. *Photograph courtesy of Andrew Grant and Neil Styles.*

Inside the church, view to the northwest. *Photograph courtesy of Andrew Grant and Neil Styles.*

The refectory. *Photograph courtesy of Andrew Grant and Neil Styles.*

the property the nuns had occupied since the 1830s—a period of time comparable to that spent by their predecessors in Cambrai.

The nettle was eventually grasped in the early years of the twenty-first century when the number of nuns at Stanbrook had fallen to just over a quarter of the number in the 1930s. The magnificent Stanbrook buildings and estate were put on the market. Abbess Joanna Jamieson, a gifted artist who had given up a promising career to become a nun in her early twenties, had the strength to see that the decision to relocate was implemented, despite the sincere misgivings of some of the nuns and the initial delay in finding a buyer for so remarkable a property.

Removal to Yorkshire

A few nuns broke from the majority of the community and set up a tiny home in East Hendred, Oxfordshire, later moving to Herefordshire. In May 2009 most of the nuns, led by their new abbess Andrea Savage, left Worcestershire by coach for their new home at Wass, in beautiful North Yorkshire moorland, where

Abbey corridors with views to the outside were designed to impress. The *via crucis* (way of the cross) corridor shown in the lower picture was provided with niches to hold carvings to depict Christ's final journey to the place of crucifixion. *Photographs courtesy of Andrew Grant and Neil Styles.*

This 1874 picture of the summer house, with a considerable gathering of people, shows gardening implements of the time. *Photograph courtesy of Stanbrook Abbey and Michael Hill.*

By the early twenty-first century the summer house had hardly changed. *Photograph courtesy of Andrew Grant and Neil Styles.*

St Mary's Retreat House was built in 1865 and was originally known as the Hermitage. *Photograph courtesy of Andrew Grant and Neil Styles.*

The design of the new abbey at Wass is markedly different from that of the community's old home at Stanbrook. *Photograph courtesy of Stanbrook Abbey.*

monasticism has a long and influential history. The area had been home to the great medieval monasteries of Rievaulx and Whitby and, much later, in 1802 the Ampleforth community arrived after being expelled from France during the Revolutionary turmoil and violence which had also been such a trauma for the Cambrai nuns. As soon as they arrived in Yorkshire the Stanbrook nuns felt welcomed by their neighbours.

Their new home, in a county steeped in religious history, has caused the nuns to return to some of the more traditional farming activities of monasticism: they somehow find time to rear livestock such as chickens and sheep in between the demands of the all-important Benedictine life of prayer and the practicalities of running the household in Yorkshire. The religious life and livestock farming have often gone hand in hand: medieval monastic communities, some on large acreages, found this an important source of income, and research has shown that the nuns at Cambrai also kept livestock.[1] At Wass, the community continues its pattern of worship, rising at 5 a.m. and attending the first service of the day—vigils—an hour later. The other services of the work of God—the opus Dei—are still faithfully attended at hours spaced out through the day until the final evening service of compline takes place at 8.15 p.m.

The name Stanbrook Abbey was retained for their new home in North Yorkshire but the modern, eco-friendly buildings, designed by the award-winning architectural practice of Fielden Clegg Bradley which also designed The Hive in Worcester, are a world away from the labour intensive and energy consuming estate the nuns left behind in Worcestershire. It has been a joy for them at last to have warm living conditions after years—in some cases a lifetime—of struggling to be comfortable in the majestic, but cold and draughty, building at Callow End which they simply could not afford to adapt to modern standards. At

1 Stanbrook archivist on 'Nuns of Yorkshire', produced by Nicola Humphries, *Open Country* (Radio Four, March 2013).

Wass there are thirty heated cells with simple en suite facilities so every sister enjoys standards which are a far cry from the basic shared facilities in their former home.

Survival

The move caused some practical anxieties, not least the fact that the Callow End property was not sold until the summer of 2010, over a year after the nuns left for Wass. It is now a luxury venue for weddings and other social and cultural events. The loss of Callow End's powerhouse of prayer and worship has been lamented by many as is inevitable with so major a change. At last, however, money is being spent on the spectacular buildings, which have been adapted to modern standards with respect both for the use for which they were originally designed and for their importance as a very significant example of the influence of E. W. Pugin.

The Stanbrook community bears the hallmarks of any institution which survives the buffeting of history and the impact of change. Survival requires courage, hard work and the ability to accept change whilst retaining a core which does not forsake those principles which formed, and still form, its *raison d'être* —the basis of its very reason for existence. In fact, Stanbrook survives in two distinct ways: not only has the Stanbrook Catholic community kept the Benedictine Rule alive in Yorkshire, but also, in Worcestershire, a now secular Stanbrook Abbey survives as a reminder of an astonishing period in architectural history.

These are indeed amazing achievements.

APPENDIX ONE
The Origins of Christian Monasticism

St Benedict of Nursia *c.* 480–*c.* 543

St Benedict, born about 480 in the mountain village of Nursia some seventy miles northeast of Rome, devised in the early sixth century a Rule for a monastic life which had a most remarkable following throughout the whole of Western Europe for the next millennium. It is still followed in religious houses to the present day. Whilst the medieval, pre-Reformation houses were all Roman Catholic, today some are Anglican though most are Roman Catholic, as is the Stanbrook Community, which moved to Wass in north Yorkshire in 2009 after over 170 years at Callow End, near Worcester. Although St Benedict's Rule has been modified to meet changing conditions and standards, the fact that it has survived for nearly fifteen centuries is a tribute to his common sense and his understanding of human nature with its spectrum of talents, hopes and frailties.

His astonishing achievement needs to be seen against the backcloth of his own time. Christianity took many years to become a significant religious movement in the face of both ridicule and cruel persecution. Its eventual acceptance by the Roman Emperor Constantine in the early fourth century was an important landmark, and by this time there had emerged Christians dedicated to practising all kinds of self-denial in their determination to commit themselves utterly to their faith.

Cenobite is the term given to those who choose to do so in communities of like-minded people, while those who choose to isolate themselves, living as hermits, are known as eremites. Among the latter a key figure was St Paul the hermit (230–343 AD) who lived in the wilderness around Thebes for about eighty years.

Some eremites demonstrated astonishing powers of endurance, possibly fired, one senses, by a somewhat unseemly spirit of competitiveness. Amongst these were the so-called pillar saints or stylites, who from the fifth century lived on tops of pillars, their name deriving from the Greek word for pillar (στυλος or stylos). This strange ascetic existence might be endured for a very long time (some say that St Simeon Stylites adopted it for thirty-seven years and St Alypius for fifty-three years) but was not a realistic goal for most people. 'Holier than thou' may seem a harsh judgement, but appears to hold some truth when studying the lives of such extraordinarily strong-willed individuals. Furthermore, some might suggest that the support system required of well-wishers supplying food and other necessary services made these loyal friends as saintly as the ascetic—indeed possibly more so. There was clearly some need for a more practical and achievable life of sacrifice, which St Benedict had the wisdom to devise in what he called his 'little Rule for beginners'.

Benedict and his sister Scholastica were the children of a wealthy Roman whose comfortable home both decided to leave in order to adopt a life style in accordance with Christian principles. Whilst, however, they disliked the pleasure-seeking and materialistic ways of Rome, they saw that compromise was possible between the excesses of town life in Rome and those of some of the ascetic eremites. It was difficult to establish communities even of very well intentioned and like-minded individuals, but Benedict spent his adult life writing and developing his Rule for those who wanted to lead a good life, such as that portrayed in the teaching of Christ, but with the recognition that the extremes of hermits and pillar saints were within neither the capability nor the wishes of many people.

The Rule Devised by St Benedict for Monastic Life

St Benedict's Rule, soon adopted in its essentials by his sister Scholastica and her followers, recommended a practical system of people living together under the authority of a spiritual father or mother (abbot or abbess). Initially there was no intention of having a wider structure or hierarchy of authority than that within the single community but such an organisation did eventually develop.

A key tenet of Benedict's Rule—recognisable down the ages to many a teacher or parent—is 'idleness is the enemy of the soul', sometimes put in the homely words of the axiom 'the devil makes work for idle hands.' So his eminently practical rule made sure that every part of the day and night was spent in some necessary or worthwhile activity, the whole idea being to achieve a balanced life. A life of prayer—several hours each day—and work of a practical or intellectual nature—normally for at least five hours each day—was to be supported by proper attention to physical needs of sleep and food which would, of course, help to optimise the quality of the work. The Benedictine term *laborare est orare* ('to work is to pray') sums up the work ethic which he advocated, seeing it as a form of offering to the God who came to be worshipped throughout the whole of Western Europe under the authority of the Pope in Rome. Practical work in fields and monastic establishments is self-evidently useful, and the intellectual achievements of monks and nuns caused many Benedictine monasteries to become centres of learning throughout the medieval period and beyond.

Each of the seventy-three chapters of the Rule was short, some very short. St Benedict, with absolute clarity, dealt with various aspects of monastic life, with particular attention to worship, conduct, diet, and care of the sick. Chapter sixteen, for example briefly set out how often services were to take place. According to Psalm 119, 'Seven times a day have I praised you,' so Benedict wrote that, 'we will fulfil this sacred number if we perform our services at lauds, prime, terce, sext, nones, vespers and compline.' But divine service did not end with these seven services because the psalmist also wrote, 'At midnight I rose to praise you,' so Benedict decreed that all his followers should also rise during the night for the service usually called *vigils*.

At the beginning of his Rule he stressed the many duties of the abbot, the most important of numerous officials. With complete control over the community the abbot, as Christ's representative, 'must know . . . however many brothers he has in his care . . . on Judgement Day he will have to submit a reckoning to God for all their souls.' On a practical level the abbot must provide the monks with everything they might need in order that the pernicious 'vice of private property' could be eradicated. Their clothing was to be decided upon by the abbot, who should distribute articles of clothing suitable for the climate and circumstances in which the community lived. No-one should complain about the colour or quality since the main requirement was that it should be easily purchased and cheap. It included items such as a tunic, a cowl (hood), stockings (if needed in a cold climate), shoes and a girdle. Basic bedding consisted of a mattress, a woollen blanket, a woollen under-blanket and a pillow. These simple beds were to be frequently searched by the abbot to ensure that no-one was hiding private property. It was 'in order that this vice of property may be cut off at the roots' that the abbot should provide everything that each monk might require, including a knife, a needle, a pen and writing tablets as well as more personal items such as a towel. The individual monk, not permitted to complain about what clothes, bedding, pens and so on that he was given, must recognise that 'distribution was made unto every man according as he had need' (Acts 4:35). Although natural weaknesses should be taken into consideration, a monk with lesser need was briskly told to thank God and not feel aggrieved; while one with greater need should show humility because of his weakness. Grumbling should not be tolerated and might well lead to punishment.

Another very important official was cellarer who had to ensure stores of food and drink were maintained—as armies are said to march on their stomachs, so did the life of prayer and work. The cellarer was to be wise, mature and humble and should 'not irritate the brothers,' though the Rule is not entirely clear as to the meaning of this. The food was to be plentiful but plain. Meat was not normally allowed but a very sick brother might be allowed it by the monk in charge of the infirmary. St Benedict thought that at the main meal, whether it was at mid-day or later, there should be, 'at all seasons, two cooked dishes . . . . Let one pound of bread suffice for a day, whether there be one principal meal or both dinner and supper.' If unusually heavy work had been required of the monks the abbot might allow something additional so long as there was no excessive indulgence for, 'above all things . . . no monk should be overtaken by indigestion.' As written in Luke 21:34, 'Take heed . . . lest . . . your hearts be overcharged with surfeiting and drunkenness and cares of this life.'

The provision of drink seems generous. 'Every man hath his proper gift from God' (1 Corinthians 7:7), so St Benedict wished to be cautious in fixing a daily allowance. 'Nevertheless, in view of the weakness of the infirm we believe that half a pint of wine a day is enough for each one. Let those to whom God gives the ability to endure abstinence know that they will have their reward.' We should, of course, see this in the context of a time when wine was of a lower alcoholic content than many of today's wines and when a supply of pure drinking water was less certain.

Silence, or restraint of speech, was one of the first matters dealt with. In chapter six we find: 'So important is silence that permission to speak should seldom be given.' It was particularly important at meal times when one of the monks would read to the rest while they were eating, taking his own meal later, though he was allowed some diluted wine before he began to read. Like the monks who sang during services, the readers would read 'according to their ability to benefit their hearers.'

Hospitality and generosity to wayfarers were seen as very important in Benedictine houses, which made a significant contribution to medieval society, giving food to the poor and to passing travellers. St Benedict thought that guests should be received in a manner such as Christ himself should be received, though he had very definite advice as to the need for an effective porter or doorkeeper, who should be 'a wise old man who shall know how to receive a reply and to return one; whose ripeness of age will not permit him to gossip.' He himself died in his sixties and perhaps it was as a young man that he formed his questionable views on the effects of age on the propensity to gossip.

Personal Demands and Widespread Effects of the Rule of St Benedict

Those who adopted the Benedictine religious life as monks or nuns took solemn vows, of which **obedience** to the Rule and to the authority of the abbot or abbess was fundamental. Personal **poverty** was another essential requirement: whilst the community owned property—some brought by those who joined the monastic house—and some communities became rich, the individual, as indicated above, had to give up private possessions and accept instead whatever food, clothing and accommodation the religious house was able and willing to provide. Benedict prescribed simple straw mattresses, plain food and monastic dress of a hooded habit and sandals. The warmth of the monastic kitchen or parlour, together with helpings of healthy food and wine became bonuses for a medieval monk, who might enjoy a more comfortable and secure living than was to be obtained outside the monastic enclosure. Benedict made clear the responsibility of the monastery to provide writing materials, a library of books and anything else that worship or work rendered necessary tools for the job. A third requirement was **chastity**, which naturally some found difficult, while for many the vow of obedience to the Rule and to the abbot or abbess will have been the most frustrating and hard to accept. But the communal monastic life was certainly pleasanter and surely more productive than life on top of a pillar or even life in the often less than salubrious or secure medieval hovel.

Benedict himself spent several years twenty-five miles from Rome at Subiaco, establishing communal life in a dozen monasteries, including that in which his sister Scholastica was abbess over a number of women. At some time about 529 he went some seventy miles southeast of Rome to Monte Cassino, where he established on the hillside a monastery revered for centuries as the birthplace of monasticism. Terrible damage was done to this historic site during fighting in the Second World War but the post-war rebuilding was impressive, even if the view towards the military cemetery on the hillside is a silent, sad reminder of how far humankind can stray from the religious ideal.

St Benedict's Rule was written down and during the middle ages was used as guidance for religious houses throughout Europe. As centuries passed it was adapted by different groups, or Orders, seeking reform of declining standards or more rigorous observance of one or other aspect of monastic life. Orders included the Cluniacs, originating in the French town of Cluny in 910 and spending so much time in worship that the contribution by lay people to work on the monastic estate was much increased. The Cistercians, originating in another

French settlement at Citeaux in Burgundy, were particularly influenced by the early twelfth-century work of St Bernard of Clairvaux and, finding no shame in getting their hands dirty, worked hard in the fields in order to maintain their life-style. Their wearing of a white choir robe over their monastic habit led to their becoming known as white monks.

Another Order, the Carthusian, was not Benedictine and emphasised the solitary aspects of monastic life which St Benedict had played down somewhat in his pursuit of a more social community. Led by St Bruno, the Carthusians were founded in 1084 and a few communities were established in England. Sometimes known as Charter Houses, they acquired this name from the original community at La Grande Chartreuse in the French Alps: they have always been particularly strict about withdrawing from society, each monk living in his own cell and meeting the rest of the community infrequently during the course of the week.

As Appendix Two shows, monasticism and the authority of the Roman Catholic Church, already under threat in some circles by the late medieval period, were to be very seriously challenged.

APPENDIX TWO
Medieval Religious Supremacy and the Rise of National Feeling

The Power of the Medieval Church in Western Europe

In medieval England the church exercised immense power, as it did in the whole of Western Europe, where people were likely to be more aware of being Christian than of belonging to a particular nation. As well as monks and nuns there were other religious groups, such as friars—Franciscan in their grey or brown habits and Dominican in black. Authority in the church was exercised by a hierarchy composed of ordained men headed by the Pope in Rome: they exercised both influence, beyond imagining by modern western democracies, over the lives of the entire population and control over vast wealth accrued from the donations of rich and poor.

None of these key clerical positions was occupied by a woman, though an abbess in charge of a community of nuns, such as that at the great Barking Abbey in Essex, would have been a force to be reckoned with. The position of women in the church reflected and reinforced the inferior status of women in society—an inequality addressed only in recent legislation in democracies and not at all in some parts of the world. Mary, mother of Christ, invoked in many prayers from men and women, particularly in time of anxiety and grief, became a significant role model for women.

Pope
Controlled the religious life of Western Europe

Archbishops
Controlled religious life throughout the provinces of Western Europe's constituent states

Bishops
Controlled bishoprics (also known as sees or dioceses) within provinces

Priests
Guided and worked closely with lay people in parishes within the bishoprics

Deacons
Often on the path to ordination as priests so had some influence in parishes

The church's hierarchical power structure as devised in medieval times

Spiritual and Material Power of the Church

The church's spiritual power was reinforced by the fact that in medieval society the clergy were usually the only people able to read and write; the church's wealth resulted from the desire—and anxieties—of people who wished to ensure divine favour not merely in the things of this world but in the hereafter in which everyone was taught to believe. Visions of eternal hell-fire were a very real threat to uneducated medieval people so generous gifts to the church were sometimes calculated attempts to buy a passage to a more desirable and congenial eternal destination. Whether the generosity sprang from genuine love of Mother Church or from calculated self-interest the result was that the Roman Catholic church in England came to own something like a third of the country's wealth, particularly in the form of land. Furthermore, educated churchmen became experts in estate management and optimised the wealth and power vested in the church.

It would, however, be wrong to forget that, even though

such concentration of power may seem dangerous to modern minds, many parish priests and other churchmen used their authority with a genuine love and concern for those in their charge: these good men believed that after death they would have to account on Judgement Day for their behaviour towards those who looked to them for guidance and support.

Challenges to the Church's Authority

The power of the church, and its stranglehold on what people should think, lasted for perhaps a thousand years. Despite the criticisms of men like John Wyclif in fourteenth-century England, it was not until the early sixteenth century that academics such as Martin Luther in Germany, John Calvin in France and Ulrich Zwingli in Switzerland effectively broke the monopoly of papal power and destroyed the old religious order for ever. Their influence came at a time when people were beginning to see themselves as belonging to a particular nation: it was no accident that the rise of nation states coincided with the decline of a church centred on the Italian city of Rome.

The destruction of the pope's authority in England by Henry VIII in the 1530s was fired by very much more than the king's desire to cast off the wife who had failed to bear him a son, and then to marry Anne Boleyn. Once a loyal Catholic to whom the Pope had given the title of Defender of the Faith, Henry became the Head of the Church in England, and thus buttressed the emerging sense of national identity which changed the European scene for ever. The authority thus assumed by Henry VIII enabled him to dissolve all the monasteries in his kingdom and take their very considerable wealth and property into his own hands. The Roman Catholic Church, attacked on several fronts by Protestant thinkers and national leaders throughout Europe, never regained the monopoly of religious power it had for centuries enjoyed in many countries. After the short reign of Henry VIII's protestant son, the boy King Edward VI, Henry's daughter Queen Mary Tudor took England back under papal control for five years. When she died her half-sister Elizabeth restored the church of her father and half-brother. Despite laws prohibiting Roman Catholicism Elizabeth had, she declared, no desire to 'make windows into men's souls'. Indeed, for the next three hundred years Catholics continued secretly to practise their religion but they were regarded with suspicion and suffered serious curtailment of civil rights until well into the nineteenth century.

Why Were Roman Catholics in England Viewed with Suspicion for Centuries?

Distrust of Roman Catholics was linked to doubts about the loyalty to the crown of those who owed allegiance to the pope—a foreign religious leader who also exercised considerable political power. Active Catholic opposition to Tudor and Stuart monarchs reached its peak with the Gunpowder Plot which so famously failed in November 1605 and served only to confirm suspicions about all things perceived as Catholic. England continued for generations to distrust anything which smacked of Roman Catholicism: one of many reasons for parliament's opposition to Charles I was his religious policy which many thought was dangerously driven by his French Roman Catholic wife and imposed by his Archbishop of Canterbury, William Laud. After the military defeats of civil war in the 1640s Charles I was tried and executed in 1649. Parliament tried for eleven years—and failed—to devise a satisfactory government without some form of leader whose powers resembled those of a king.

Refusal to Accept a Roman Catholic Monarch

Republicanism having failed, Charles I's son was welcomed back in 1660 as Charles II, astute enough to hide his Catholic leanings and so to die peacefully in his bed in 1685. His brother James II, lacking the skills necessary for political survival, effectively disqualified himself from the role of monarch by his overt support of the faith so feared by his subjects. The throne was offered to his daughter Mary II and her husband William III, who was also her cousin. Both William and Mary were Protestant and ruled as joint monarchs, though Mary died of smallpox in 1694 and William reigned alone until his death in 1702, when he was succeeded by Mary's sister, Anne, who died in 1714 leaving no direct heir, having lost every one of the many children she bore. Her nearest Protestant relative and heir was the German Elector of Hanover, whose imperfect command of English did not prevent his effective rule as king of England from 1714 until his death in 1727. He was, however, challenged early in his reign by James Edward Stuart, nicknamed the Old Pretender, who was the Roman Catholic son of the deposed James II.

The Jacobites

Attempts in 1715 and 1745 to restore James Edward Stuart to the throne are known as the Jacobite risings. The Old Pretender and, to an even greater extent, his son Bonnie Prince Charlie, have acquired a romantic image, but the activities of their followers meant that during the eighteenth century fear of Roman Catholics continued to be a significant feature of domestic politics. The Jacobite rebellions reinforced in many people's minds the need for legislation which deprived Roman Catholics of numerous civil rights. This in turn led Roman Catholics, unhappy with their treatment, to seek to maintain in secret the religion which they cherished—a dangerous undertaking which could lead to harsh punishment. At last, in 1829 the Catholic Emancipation Act enabled them to come out from hiding, enjoy the same civil liberties as the rest of the population and take up public office as well as the teaching and military posts which had been unavailable to them. There remained, however, considerable unease about the rituals of their religious practices, exacerbated by the 1870 declaration of papal infallibility. The path to religious toleration was full of stumbling blocks on all sides.

Some knowledge of these events is necessary for an understanding of three centuries of distrust and antipathy towards Roman Catholics and of the reasons why it was unrealistic to seek to found a new Roman Catholic monastic community in England during those three centuries. The nuns who came to Stanbrook in the 1830s, after surviving in the 1790s a life and death struggle in the horrors of the French Revolution, managed to achieve an apparently impossible feat.

GLOSSARY

abbey. A religious house with considerable autonomy in which monks or nuns follow the rules of their order.

abbot or abbess. The head of an abbey.

antiphon. Musical setting of texts in which two persons or groups respond to each other in church services.

Benedictine. Following the teaching of St Benedict of Nursia (*c.* 480–*c.* 547).

breviary. Book containing the requirements of the daily services, prayers, texts etc.

Carmelite. Following teaching which originated at about 1200 AD at Mount Carmel in Palestine, with particular emphasis on contemplation and respect for Mary, mother of Christ.

cellarer. The holder of a key position of responsibility in charge of supplies of food and drink in a religious house (see Obedientaries).

cenobite. One who practises a religious vocation in company with others, as in a monastery. St Benedict considered this the best way to follow a vocation to a religious life.

Carthusians. Founded at Chartreuse near Grenoble by St Bruno in 1084, this order adapted the ideas of St Benedict and others, seeking a contemplative life rather different from the Benedictine pattern.

Cluniacs. Founded at Cluny in 910, this order sought a return to a strict adhesion to the Rule of St Benedict, placing emphasis on fine churches and seeking to avoid secular influence on monastic life.

Cistercians. Founded in 1098 at Cîteaux, this order sought a return to a strict adhesion to the Rule of St Benedict, placing greater emphasis on simplicity and manual labour.

confession or penance. A sacrament mainly used in the Roman Catholic Church in which penitents confess their sins to a priest in private and he, bound by the church to keep secret anything he learns in the Confession, pronounces forgiveness and possibly an appropriate penance. Sometimes referred to more specifically as auricular confession.

convent. Modern usage tends to use this word for a house of nuns but in fact it is applicable to any abbey.

Dame. The title given to a professed nun in certain orders.

Dom. The title given to a professed monk in certain orders.

English Benedictine Congregation (EBC). An association of Benedictine monasteries, all of which follow the Rule of St Benedict but maintain their autonomy.

eremite. One who practises a religious vocation in isolation (a hermit).

Gregorian chant. Introduced in the sixth century and attributed (possibly wrongly) to Pope Gregory I (*c.* 540–604), this style of music, used for church services, was also known as plainsong. It has been developed and embellished over many centuries during which it became a central characteristic of Roman Catholic worship and of some other Christian denominations. In modern times it has also enjoyed something of a cult following by lay persons.

hours. Services in the monastic day held at set times and including readings often with plainsong rendering of psalms, prayers and hymns. St Benedict decreed that there should be seven such services during the day and an additional one during the night. Some religious houses, including Stanbrook, have modified these requirements but retain the essential spirit of regular and frequent worship every day. In addition the Mass or Holy Communion was held on certain days, especially the great feasts of the Christian year such as Christmas or Easter. The eight original services were known as the offices and consisted of:

matins (also called vigils, the night office or nocturn and held during the night).

lauds (morning prayer, at dawn or during the night).

prime (at the first hour—about 6 a.m.).

terce (at the third hour—about 9 a.m.).

sext (at the sixth hour, about noon).

none (at the ninth hour, mid-afternoon).

vespers (evening prayer, about 6 p.m.).

compline (about 9 p.m.).

infirmarian. Responsible for the care of sick brethren and for the regular blood-letting, or 'cupping' believed in medieval times to be necessary for the maintenance of good health.

lay brothers and sisters. Members of a monastic community sharing in its life and work but without taking the full vows of a professed monk or nun.

Lectio divina. Reading and meditation on religious writing forming part of the discipline of the monastic rule.

lectionary. Book of scriptural readings.

liturgy. The ritual of services.

Mass. The most solemn service of the Roman Catholic faith in memory of the last supper taken by Christ with his disciples before his crucifixion

monastery. A religious house for monks or nuns (though in more recent times there has developed a tendency to use the terms nunnery or convent for the homes of the latter).

obedientaries. The monks/nuns appointed to take charge, under the abbot or abbess to whom they owed obedience, of particular aspects of monastic life, e.g. the Cellarer, Infirmarian, Precentor etc.

offices. See hours.

order. A group of religious following a specific version of monastic life. See Carthusian, Cistercian, Cluniac.

plainsong. Another name for Gregorian chant.

postulant. One who wishes to adopt the religious life.

precentor. In charge of music for services and often also of books and the monastic library.

priest. Always male in the Roman Catholic Church, a priest has the authority to take sacraments such as the Mass or the hearing of confessions.

priory. A monastic house subservient to (or daughter house of) an abbey (mother house) in which the head is known as prior or prioress.

profession. The ceremony at which a man or woman takes monastic vows.

psalter. Book of Psalms.

sacrament. One of seven rites to which spiritual importance is attached. In the Roman Catholic church the seven sacraments are baptism, confession (penance), confirmation, Holy Communion (Mass), marriage, ordination of priests and deacons, and extreme unction (when death seems imminent). All normally require an ordained priest, though baptism can, in life-threatening emergency after childbirth, be performed for an infant without a priest being present.

vows. The three vows commonly taken by monks and nuns are those of:

poverty: (although private property has always been forbidden, the house or order have sometimes become rich).

chastity: any special relationships are seen as detracting from the special relationship desirable between God and the individual and so must be avoided.

obedience: individual preference must, according to the Rule of St Benedict, yield to the instructions of the abbot or abbess in the interest of the community.

BIBLIOGRAPHY

Bantoft, Arthur. 'The Gascoigne Family and the Catholic Church in the 17th and 18th Centuries', *The Barwicker*, No. 69 (March 2003). Available at http://www.barwickinelmethistoricalsociety.com/6908.html

Benedictines of Stanbrook. *In a Great Tradition* (John Murray, 1956).

The Bible (Authorised Version of 1611).

Blunt, Wilfrid. *Cockerell* (Alfred A. Knopf, 1964).

British Listed Buildings Online: http://www.britishlistedbuildings.co.uk/stanbrookabbey

Bush, William. *To Quell the Terror,* (ICS Publications, 1999).

Card, Revd. Henry. *Antiquities of the Priory of Great Malvern* (Rivington, London, 1834).

Champ, Judith. 'William Ullathorne'. Paper given in 1985 at the English Benedictine Congregation History Commission Symposium. Colwich Abbey website, http://www.colwichabbey.org.uk

Corrigan, Felicitas. *Friends of a Lifetime: Nun, the Infidel and the Superman* (Fount, 1990).

Guilday, Revd. Peter. *The English Catholic Refugees on the Continent 1558–1795*, vol. 1 (Longmans, Green and Co., 1914).

Edwards, Dame Eanswythe. 'The Influence on the English Benedictine Congregation of Dom Gueranger's Revival.' A paper given in 1975 at the English Benedictine Congregation History Commission Symposium.

Edwards, Dame Eanswythe. 'Home at Last'. A short account of the community's history until its move to Stanbrook in a paper given in 1988 to commemorate 150 years at Stanbrook.

Encyclopaedia Britannica Online, s.v. 'Reign of Terror,' http://www.britannica.com/event/Reign-of-Terror.

Fort, Gertrud von le. *A Song at the Scaffold* (Sheed and Ward, 1933).

Fry, Timothy. *The Rule of St Benedict in English* (The Liturgical Press, Minnesota, 1982).

Gateacre Society Records: http://www.liverpool.ndo.co.uk/gatsoc/news06/page15.html

Grant, Andrew. 'Stanbrook Abbey, Callow End, Worcestershire, sale brochure' (2009).

Heywood, Cecilia. 'Records of the English Benedictine Nuns at Cambrai 1620–1793', in Catholic Record Society's *Miscellanea*, vol. VIII (1913)

Hill, Michael. 'Conservation Plan for Stanbrook Abbey' (2005).

Hill, Rosemary. *God's Architect* (Allen Lane, 2007).

Hurle, Pamela. *Castlemorton Farmer; John Rayer Lane 1798–1871* (Pamela Hurle, 1996).

Hyland, G. J. 'Chronological Gazetteer of the Works of E. E. Pugin' http://www.thepuginsociety.co.uk/convent-chapels.html

Lunn, David. *The English Benedictines 1540–1688* (Burns and Oates, 1980).

McLachlan, Dame Laurentia. *Stanbrook Abbey; A Sketch of its History* (Burns, Oates and Washbourne, 1925).

Mark, Helen. 'Nuns of Yorkshire', produced by Nicola Humphries, *Open Country* (Radio Four, March 2013).

Mawer, A., F. M. Stenton and F. T. S. Houghton. *The Place-Names of Worcestershire* (C.U.P. 1969).

Meisel, Antony and M. L. Del Mastro. *The Rule of St Benedict* (Image/Doubleday, 1975).

Oxford Dictionary of National Biography, online, http://www.oxforddnb.com

Partington, Ann Theresa. Catholic Record Society, *Miscellanea*, vol. VIII. Account as transcribed.

Pevsner Nikolaus. *The Buildings of England, Worcestershire* (Penguin, 1977).

Read, Piers Paul. *Alec Guinness: The Authorised Biography* (Simon and Schuster, 2003).

Roberts, John Stuart. *Siegfried Sassoon* (Richard Cohen Books, 1999).

The Tablet, various issues, as shown in footnotes.

Sandeman, Dame Frideswide. *Dame Gertrude More* (Gracewing, Fowler Wright Books, 1997).

Sandeman, Dame Frideswide. 'Laurence Shepherd, 1825–85, Apostle of Gueranger', *Ampleforth Journal* (1975).

Stanbrook Abbey website: http://www.stanbrookabbey.org.uk

Waddell, Helen. *The Desert Fathers* (Constable, 1974).

Whitemore, Hugh. *The Best of Friends* (Amber Lane Press, 1988).

Wolfe, Heather. 'Cambrai's Imprint on the Life of Lady Falkland'. Paper given in 1998 at the English Benedictine Congregation History Commission Symposium.

Yorkshire Life (20 December 2010).

LITERARY WORKS ASSOCIATED WITH THE LIFE AND WORK OF THE STANBROOK COMMUNITY

Godden, Rumer, *In This House of Brede* (Macmillan, 1969; (Pan, 1970).
Murdoch, Iris, *The Bell* (Chatto and Windus, 1973; Vintage, 1999).
Sassoon, Siegfried, *The Path to Peace* (Stanbrook Press, 1960).